THE MOST POPULAR
ITALIAN COOKBOOK IN AMERICA

With this book, you can easily duplicate the wonderful dishes that the author's grandmother turned out in her vast kitchen in Italy where Maria Lo Pinto learned the art of Italian cooking.

This is the basic book for cooks who want to produce the savory, mouth-watering traditional dishes of sunny Italy. It covers everything from hearty pasta to lighter-than-air desserts. It tells you how to use the age-old components—pungent garlic; bland olive oil; red, juicy tomatoes; subtle mushrooms; tangy cheeses; the piquant herbs, oregano and basil—that are the heart of Italian cooking.

THE ART OF ITALIAN COOKING

D1013501

Other Bantam Cookbooks
Ask your bookseller for the books you have missed

AMERICA'S FAVORITE RECIPES FROM BETTER HOMES AND GARDENS
THE ART OF BARBECUE AND OUTDOOR COOKING
THE ART OF FISH COOKING
THE ART OF FRENCH COOKING
THE ART OF GERMAN COOKING
THE COMPLETE BOOK OF MEXICAN COOKING
THE COMPLETE BOOK OF WINE COOKERY
THE ALL-NEW FANNIE FARMER BOSTON COOKING SCHOOL COOKBOOK
THE FANNIE FARMER JUNIOR COOKBOOK
THE HAWAII COOKBOOK AND BACKYARD LUAU
AN HERB AND SPICE COOK BOOK
HORS D'OEUVRE AND CANAPES
THE ART OF ITALIAN COOKING
THE ART OF JEWISH COOKING
THE COMPLETE BOOK OF ORIENTAL COOKING
THE SPANISH COOKBOOK
THE COMPLETE BOOK OF VEGETABLE COOKERY
THE TUESDAY SOUL FOOD COOKBOOK
BETTER HOMES AND GARDENS CASSEROLE COOKBOOK
THE DRINKING MAN'S DIET COOKBOOK
THE PANCAKE COOKBOOK

The Art of Italian Cooking

by Maria Lo Pinto
and Milo Miloradovich

This low-priced Bantam Book has been completely reset in a type face designed for easy reading, and was printed from new plates. It contains the complete text of the original hard-cover edition.
NOT ONE WORD HAS BEEN OMITTED.

THE ART OF ITALIAN COOKING
A Bantam Book / published by arrangement with Doubleday & Company, Inc.

PRINTING HISTORY

Doubleday edition published March 1948
2nd printing ..... May 1948 *5th printing ..... January 1950*
3rd printing ... December 1948 *6th printing ..... June 1952*
4th printing ..... April 1949 *7th printing ..... October 1953*
8th printing ..... March 1955

Bantam edition published October 1955
2nd printing ..... October 1955 *6th printing ... December 1956*
3rd printing ... November 1955 *7th printing ..... January 1958*
4th printing .... February 1956 *8th printing .... February 1959*
5th printing ..... May 1956 *9th printing ... December 1959*
10th printing .... February 1961

Bantam Reference Library edition published March 1962
12th printing ... February 1963 *13th printing .... January 1964*
14th printing ... November 1964

Bantam Cookbook Shelf edition published October 1965
16th printing ..... July 1966 *20th printing ..... May 1968*
17th printing ..... March 1967 *21st printing ..... August 1968*
18th printing .... October 1967 *22nd printing .... October 1968*
19th printing ..... April 1968 *23rd printing ..... July 1969*
24th printing ..... October 1969

All rights reserved.
Copyright 1948 by Doubleday & Company, Inc.
This book may not be reproduced in whole or in part, by mimeograph or any other means, without permission.
For information address: Doubleday & Company, Inc., 277 Park Avenue, New York, N.Y. 10017.

Published simultaneously in the United States and Canada

Bantam Books are published by Bantam Books, Inc., a National General company. Its trade-mark, consisting of the words "Bantam Books" and the portrayal of a bantam, is registered in the United States Patent Office and in other countries. Marca Registrada. Bantam Books, Inc., 666 Fifth Avenue, New York, N.Y. 10019.

PRINTED IN THE UNITED STATES OF AMERICA

In Appreciation

MY DEEP APPRECIATION GOES TO MY SISTERS FRANCES, Sophie, Josephine, and Rose for their inspiring encouragement and assistance in preparing and checking these recipes used by our mother and grandmother: "Nonni."

Special thanks are given my aunts, Lena Occhipinti, Fanny Di Peri, Tessie Lupo, Sophie Natoli, Concetta Barbara, Cousin Mary Terranova, and cousins Mario and Dan; and to "Mama" Bonaccolto and Uncle Vincent for their loving interest and warm generosity in contributing special family recipes.

MARIA LO PINTO

Foreword

AT HOME, THERE WERE ALWAYS SIXTEEN OR EIGHTEEN persons seated at table. It was never necessary to warn the cook, hours ahead of time, that a member of the family was bringing a guest to dinner. Invariably there was sufficient food for one or two additional persons. In fact, the unexpected guest became almost a tradition in our household.

The enthusiastic appreciation of our guests and the unstinting praise of our intimate friends inspired this special book. Over and over they would exclaim and ask: "How do you cook that?" or: "What ingredients did you use to make this so palatably light and delicious?"

These repeated questions and praise made all of us ponder the great treasure of recipes that was ours. Many had been in the family for generations and had seldom, if ever, been made known outside Nonni's kitchen.

These suggestions and directions have been prepared for all those persons who pride themselves in serving the "out of the ordinary" in food. It may be just one unusual recipe for which you are searching, or it may be an entire meal that appeals to your desire to experiment with and serve new and unusual food. Whatever your cooking inclinations may be, this book is arranged in the sequence of a complete menu, making it easy to plan unique combinations. You may select a single favorite recipe from each section, beginning with antipasto and ending with *caffe espresso* (black coffe), and find you have planned your own individual menu.

Don't fear "trying out" something different for your family and friends. All good cooking—whether it be French, American, Spanish, or Italian—requires that extra bit of "liking," a little experimenting with the exact amount of "salt to taste." The good cook learns through experience that some vegetables taste better with slightly more salt, some with a little less.

It is just the same with these recipes. After using them once or twice you will begin to sense the exact quantity of seasoning that suits your family's palate. In other words, with a reasonable degree of patience you can bring out the rare and pungent flavors of the many combinations suggested in this collection. Your reward will be satisfying and, more than this, it will be unusual, for Italian food, carefully prepared, is just that.

This book is dedicated to you—to all of you who enjoy and appreciate the unusual in unusual food.

MARIA LO PINTO

Contents

In Appreciation V

Foreword VII

Quotation XI

INTRODUCTION

1. *Nonni's Kitchen—Oil, Herbs, Cheese, Pasta* 1
2. *Wines, Customs, and Festivals* 12
3. *Festival Menus* 20
4. *Salute! Dinner Begins with Antipasto* 28

RECIPES

5. *Soups* 33
6. *Spaghetti and Pasta* 40
7. *Sauces* 53
8. *Sea Foods* 58
9. *Meats* 74
10. *Vegetables and Salads* 93
11. *Game and Fowl* 110
12. *Desserts* 122
13. *Luncheon Delicacies* 139
14. *Glossary of Italian Terms* 151

Standard Measurements 158

Index 161

Introduction

Eat thy bread with joy, and
drink thy wine with a merry heart.

ECCLESIASTES IX:7

CHAPTER ONE

Nonni's Kitchen

OIL—HERBS—CHEESE—PASTA

SAVORY, SPICY AROMAS FILLED EVERY CORNER OF THE LOWER floor at Nonni's. Without a doubt, Grandmother, whom we all affectionately called "Nonni," was cooking one of her special sauces. Her kitchen was a wonderland to us, and when we behaved ourselves Nonni would let us watch her blend the oils and herbs that made her sauces better than anyone else's in all the world.

The red coals were usually smoldering in the large gray fieldstone oven which occupied one corner of Nonni's spacious kitchen in her home in Marineo, a little village near Palermo. We had always been interested in that room —ever since we were big enough to toddle in to ask Nonni for hot cookies or some tasty little tidbits to nibble. The huge oven intrigued us, and we loved to watch Nonni or the cook open the center baking compartment of the triangular top which formed a chimney. When this happened, we knew there was something delicious about to be taken out and tasted.

A large stone extension formed the top of the stove and had an open grate over the center where meats were broiled. Usually there was a shiny copper pan or two standing to one side or back of the grate. It would be filled with simmering tomato or clam sauce. We learned then that the longer and more slowly a sauce simmered the better its flavor.

The lower part of the spacious oven or stove was used as a storage place for both wood and coal. We often used to bring in twigs from the nearby woodland and pack them in systematic rows beside the coal, so that Nonni's supply was never low. Our reward was a handful of *pignoli* (pine nuts) or an extra cookie.

The kitchen was at least twenty-four feet square with a bright red tile floor bordered in gay yellow, orange, and green. The sunlight streaming in through the two huge windows and open doorway revealed walls and a beamed ceiling that were snowy white.

Terra-cotta and clay casseroles, used for baking *lasagne imbottite* (stuffed noodles) or for marinating game and fish, were standing in neat rows on wooden shelves along one wall. On the opposite wall, large and small copper pots and pans hung in neat rows, awaiting the eager and expert hands of Nonni or the cook. Nonni not only loved to choose just the right pan for each special dish, but she knew how important that choice could be to the ultimate success of her cooking.

Alongside this bright display were long-handled wooden forks and spoons, in addition to copper ones of various sizes and shapes. They were all within easy reach for this dainty little woman who insisted upon doing most of the cooking herself. Though the cook was always busy, it was Nonni who supervised the special preparations and planned all the meals.

Old Italian kitchen cabinets lined the other wall. One held the smaller kitchen utensils and china and the other was filled with kitchen linens and glassware.

Water and wine jugs made of terra cotta stood on two small tables. Each one would have made a beautiful study in still life. The water jugs were more than mere decorations. They were a necessity, because in those years Nonni had none of the conveniences of our modern kitchens. All the water had to be carried from the family wells, which were about two city blocks distant. There was a small cement outlet or drain in the kitchen floor which carried away all the waste.

We loved the massive hand-hewn walnut table which stood at the other end of the kitchen. Sixteen or more of us could enjoy the gaiety of an evening meal in the warm informality of Nonni's company whenever we wished. The brightly lighted brass lamps and the candles burning in the shining copper or majolica candlesticks lent a decorative air to the whole place. The memory of the warm joy of those long evening meals—really almost parties to us—fills us with nostalgia whenever we talk about them.

We see again the picturesque setting, lighted by the old lamp and the burning candles. They often flickered out before we reluctantly left to go to our own rooms. We smell once more the delicious aroma of Nonni's pungent sauces and wonder what it was that made all her cooking so different. Was it only her skillful blending of oils and herbs, or was it her loving and careful preparation?

OLIVE OIL

Olive oil and herbs are used in practically every Italian recipe. However, in northern Italy many cooks prefer to use butter, though an extra drop of oil in this or that combination adds an indefinable distinction of flavor.

There is a legend that an olive grove, planted by the ancient Greeks and Saracens, still grows in Sicily. Though they were the first peoples to introduce the olive trees into southern Italy, it is doubtful whether any of those ancient gnarled trunks still remain.

There are two species of trees: the low gnarled type with willow-like leaves and the poplar-shaped tree, tall and slender. The olive tree is ten years old before it begins to bear the precious olive-green fruit. From then on it continues to produce for generations.

The black ripe olive is used only for eating. It is either dried in the sun and cured with salt and olive oil, or it is preserved in brine. The green species is the olive from which the oil is extracted. The crop is harvested about the middle of November. After crushing and pressing the fruit the oil is graded and distributed for home and export consumption.

The owners of large olive groves often have their own crushing and pressing machinery. The old-fashioned crusher resembles the ancient hand-operated corn press of the Philistines. It is much like the press or mill which Samson wearily turns in the opera *Samson and Delilah.* The crusher consists of a large circular vat about fifteen feet in diameter, covered by a platform on which a heavy stone wheel revolves. A long horizontal bar is attached to the wheel which crushes the olives and pits as it revolves.

A patient, blindfolded little donkey is hitched to the bar, and as he walks round and round the platform, the wheel compresses the pits and olives into a conglomerate mass ready for the next process of pressing. The little animal covers several miles in his monotonous journey, and attendants often have to urge him to go on. They also watch the crushing process and continuously push the crushed mixture toward the center of the platform so that all pulp will be equally distributed and evenly crushed.

The olive pulp is then placed in large, square, porous baskets made of straw or hemp. When filled with pulp, packed ready for pressing, the baskets resemble bales of cotton. The bales are piled in tiers of six each and carefully clamped together with an iron press at the top and bottom. Each tier is then placed over a huge cement vat sunk into the ground. As the pressure of the clamps is increased, by turning an iron rod, the oil oozes down into the vats. Each vat holds about one hundred gallons of the precious liquid. When the sluggish drip-drip has finally filled the vats, the oil is ladled out layer by layer and graded.

The top layer is considered the finest quality and is called "virgin oil." The next layer is then carefully ladled out and graded. It is somewhat heavier than the first layer. This process continues until all oil has been removed and nothing is left but a dark, thick, watery residue.

Sometimes this cloudy substance is burned as a light. First it is mixed with a small amount of heavy crude olive oil and poured into a short, thick glass. Then a wick is inserted and, when lighted, produces a flame much brighter than that of an ordinary wax candle.

Should the owner of a small grove have no press of his own, there is always a public press where he may send his fruit to be crushed. His share of oil is returned to him, having been graded and measured, olive for olive. Many times the owner supplies his own containers for the family's share of oil. If no clay jars are available and he is particularly enterprising, he may slaughter and skin a goat. After the skin has been sterilized and cured, it is sewn up and used to hold the oil. The natural form is not destroyed, and when completed it looks like a small edition of a Tony Sarg balloon. The goatskin, filled with oil, closely resembles the little billy goat before his pelt became a convenient container.

While this old-fashioned crushing and pressing process still goes on in many of the small towns and villages, modern machinery has now replaced the patient little donkey.

HERBS IN ITALIAN COOKING

A volume might easily be devoted to the history of herbs, but only those most frequently used in Italian cooking are mentioned here. The use of herbs—as the use of other seasoning—is one that grows to be highly individual. In the beginning it is good to be over-cautious and to use a smaller quantity rather than more, until you discover the subtle flavoring effect of each herb.

It is interesting to experiment with combinations of two or three different herbs. You will find that they add a "certain something" to salads as well as to cooked foods and impart a new and unusual flavor to your cookery.

The herbs included in these recipes are the favorites which made Nonni's cooking so distinctly characteristic and individual.

HERBS

AGLIO—Garlic: A bulb, which has a characteristic strong scent and pungent flavor, composed of a number of smaller bulbs called cloves. Used in flavoring meats, sauces, vegetables, and salad dressings.

ANETO—Dill: A European herb used with its seeds for flavoring pickles. Fresh leaves sometimes used in salads.

ANICE—Aniseed: Sometimes called fennel seed. The aromatic seeds of a perennial plant having yellow flowers and finely divided leaves. Used in condiments, sausages, and sauce. The oil of the seed is used in flavoring pastries, and the liqueur called anisette.

BASILICO—Basil: A variety of sweet green leaf of delicate flavor belonging to the mountain mint species; mildly fragrant. Used in flavoring soups, stews, vegetables, fowl, meats, and sauces.

CANNELLA—Cinnamon: Highly aromatic bark used in powder or stick form. Used in flavoring desserts. Sometimes used in stuffings.

CAPPERI—Capers: Greenish flower buds of caper plant in brine. Used chiefly in salads and fish sauces.

CHIODI DI GAROFONI—Cloves: The dried flower bud of a myrtaceous tree. Used whole or ground as a very pungent aromatic spice in flavoring meats and game.

CIPOLLA—Onion: The bulb of a garden plant having a strong characteristic flavor and odor. Used quite universally in cookery.

FOGLIE DI ALLORO—Bay Leaves: The aromatic leaf of a shrub resembling laurel. Used in stews, sauces, and game dishes.

MAGGIORANA—Marjoram: The ground common sweet marjoram (a genus of aromatic mint) is very fragrant and adds a spicy flavor. Sometimes used instead of sage in sauces and stuffings.

MENTA—Mint: An aromatic herb of the genus *Mentha,* used in flavoring lamb, fowl, vegetables, condiments, and salad dressings.

NOCE MOSCATA—Nutmeg: A seed enclosed in the pear-shaped fruit of the nutmeg tree. When ground, the nutmeg is strongly fragrant. Used chiefly in desserts, and sometimes in stuffings.

OREGANO—Orégano: Leaves of an aromatic shrub somewhat more delicate than thyme. Used in flavoring sauces, salads, meats, and fowl.

PEPE FORTE – Crushed Red Pepper Seeds: Dried, crushed, hot red garden pepper with seeds.

PREZZEMOLO—Parsley: A European garden herb, commonly used to flavor soups, fish, stuffings, and stews; or as a garnish.

ROSAMARINA—Rosemary: A warm, pungent shrub with a bitter taste which changes to a delicate flavor after cooking. Generally used with veal, lamb, fish, and fowl.

SALVIA—Sage: A pungent, minty, grayish-green aromatic herb. Used in flavoring stuffings, meats, and fowl.

TIMO—Thyme: The common garden species has mild, spicy, tiny leaves. Used quite generally in soups, sauces, salads, meats, fowl, and game.

ZAFFERANO—Saffron: Dried orange-colored stigmas of the saffron plant. One ounce requires more than 4000 flowers. The powder is used as a mild flavoring in soups and sauces as well as for its color.

CHEESE

Cheese, too, is used so extensively in all Italian kitchens that this list is included as a guide to assist you in becoming more familiar with the various types. All these can be easily purchased in practically every retail cheese store. You will soon become acquainted with the various mild or sharp flavors and will learn to identify the kinds used for grating and those for slicing.

BEL PAESE: Mild, soft, pale yellow cheese, noted for its delicacy. Round heads weigh about 5 lbs. each.

CACIOCAVALLO: Sicilian cheese. Yellow, hard texture; has a spicy, tangy flavor. Eaten sliced. When properly aged, may be grated for use as seasoning. Oblong loaves; about 20 inches long and 7 inches square.

GORGONZOLA: Very pungent, highly flavored, creamy-white, flaked with green mold, as is Roquefort cheese. Eaten sliced or crumbled for use as flavoring in salad dressings.

INCANESTRATO: Sicilian grating cheese (made from cow's and goat's milk combined). Used as seasoning. Very sharp and white; sometimes contains whole black pepper. Large round heads weigh about 15 to 20 lbs.

MANTECA: A combination of cheese and butter. The small brick of butter is covered with Mozzarella. Eaten sliced. Not a cooking cheese.

MOZZARELLA: A moist, smooth, white, unsalted cheese; about size of large cup. Not spicy; for use in baking as well as eating.

MOZZARELLA - AFFUMICATA: Smoked Mozzarella sometimes called "Scamozza." Eaten sliced only.

PARMIGIANO: A yellow, mild, dry cheese known as "Parmesan"; usually grated for use as seasoning.

PECORINO: Off-white, medium-sharp goat's-milk grating cheese. Used as seasoning.

PROVOLONE: Mild, rather hard-texture slicing cheese. Light yellow; molded into small balls weighing about 4 lbs. Also shaped like a large bologna weighing about 6 to 8 lbs.

RICOTTA: A fresh, moist, unsalted cottage cheese for cooking and pastries. Also used very much like cream cheese in sandwiches and salads.

RICOTTA SALATA: Salty, dry, hard ricotta; usually grated for use as seasoning. Rather mild.

ROMANO: Off-white grating cheese used for flavoring. Made from cow's and goat's milk combined. Sharp, tangy flavor.

SCAMOZZA: Smooth, white, unsalted, pear-shaped cheese; eaten sliced.

STRACHINO: Very sharp light yellow goat's-milk cheese; eaten sliced; never grated.

PASTA

Pasta—Types of Macaroni—Often Used in Italian Cooking

"Pasta" identifies any type paste made from wheat flour. It is dried in various shapes and forms, each one of which is given a descriptive name. Pasta—in some form—is a regular part of the daily Italian menu and is served in a great variety of interesting and tempting ways. Italian grocery stores carry all types of pasta, and those most commonly used in cooking are listed here.

ACINI DI PEPE: Tiny pieces of round or square pasta called "pepper kernels" because they resemble them and are less than 1/32 inch in size.

CAPPELLETTI: Freshly prepared moist pasta shaped like "little hats"; usually filled with chopped chicken.

CAVATONI RIGATI: A ribbed, curved, tubular pasta about 2 inches long and ½ inch in diameter.

CONCHIGLIE: Pasta shaped like little sea shells. Sometimes called "maruzzelle."

DITALI: Pasta dried in tubular form about ¼ inch in diameter and ½ inch long.

DITALINI: Same shape as ditali but cut in ¼-inch lengths. Used in *minestras* and soups.

FARFALLETTE: A decorative pasta shaped into small and large ribbon bows. Sometimes called "butterflies."

FUSILLI: A spiral, curly spaghetti.

LASAGNE: Egg or plain noodles cut in medium and wide widths.

LINGUINI: Narrow, plain noodles about ⅛ inch wide.

MAFALDE: Long, twisted ribbon noodles.

MEZZANI: A smooth, curved, tubular pasta about 1 inch long and ¼ inch in diameter.

MOSTACCIOLI: Smooth, tubular, very hollow pasta, cut obliquely in 2½ inch lengths, about ½ inch in diameter.

PASTINA: Tiny pasta disks about ⅛ inch in diameter; used only in soups.

PASTINA AL UOVO: Shaped like pastina, but made with eggs.

PERCIATELLI: Long, tubular pasta; more hollow and slightly larger in diameter than spaghetti.

RAVIOLI: Freshly prepared, moist, very thin pasta, about 2 inches square; filled with chopped chicken, spinach, meat, or ricotta.

RIGATONI: Large, ribbed, tubular pasta cut into 3-inch lengths.

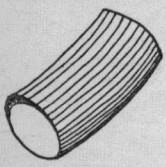

SPAGHETTI: A wheat-flour pasta dried in long, thin, tubular lengths.

SPAGHETTINI: Very thin spaghetti; not quite as slender as vermicelli.

TAGLIARINI: Very narrow egg noodles about 1/8 inch wide.

TUBETTINI: Tiny tubes of pasta cut into 1/8-inch lengths; used only in soups or *minestras.*

VERMICELLI: Angel hair, very thin spaghetti. Usually dried separately like spaghetti; however, sometimes 15 or 20 strands are twisted to resemble a bowknot.

ZITI: Plain, tubular pasta about 3 inches long and 1/2 inch in diameter.

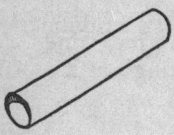

CHAPTER TWO

Wines, Customs, and Festivals

WINES

IN EVERY ITALIAN HOUSEHOLD WINE TAKES THE PLACE OF drinking water. Usually a mild burgundy or chianti is served with every dinner. Drinking tart red wine is as important to the full enjoyment of eating pasta as is a good sauce.

The best chefs in the world have always used wines for flavoring, and none will deny that the correct wines, wisely served, add an indescribable charm to even the most simple meal.

Wine also has its own food value as well as flavor. Webster defines *food* as "anything that nourishes or sustains." So returning to our early lessons in nutrition, we can search for the carbohydrates and calories. Those in wine are hidden in the alcoholic content. One gram of alcohol contains more calories than an equal amount of carbohydrates, but less calories than are found in one gram of fat.

The drier red wines such as burgundy, claret, and chianti, served so often with Italian food, contain only half the calories found in the sweet wines such as port, sherry, muscatel, and tokay. If, therefore, wines are included in the menu, their actual food value should also be considered.

The proper choice of wines, as the choice of other flavoring, is something that must be acquired through patience and experience. If after experimenting you discover that your family prefers a fuller, fruitier wine than claret with spaghetti, then remember to serve chianti, zinfandel, or burgundy. There are numerous pamphlets and books from which one may learn the correct order of serving wines. Perhaps this list will be helpful to those who are just beginning to discover the many domestic wines that are plentiful and not expensive.

CORRECT ORDER OF SERVING WINES:

Course	*Wine*	*Temperature*
Antipasto	Pale dry sherry	Well chilled
	Old sherry	" "
	Dry white port	Chilled
	Dry vermouth	"
	Sweet vermouth	"
Oysters Shrimps	Rhine wine	"
Fish	Sauterne, medium or dry and haut	Well chilled
	Chablis	" "
	Riesling	" "
Soup	Old sherry	" "
	Pale dry sherry	" "
Spaghetti, Ravioli	Chianti	Chilled
Red Meats and Game	Burgundy	Chilled
	Claret	"
	Zinfandel	"
	Bordeaux	Well chilled
White Meats and Fowl	Chablis	" "
	Riesling	" "
	Rhine wine	" "
	Sauterne	" "
	Moselle	" "
Salad	All dry white wines	" "
Dessert	Sparkling burgundy	" "
	Champagne	" "
	Sparkling moselle	" "

Course	*Wine*	*Temperature*
Dessert	Asti Spumanti (Italian champagne)	Well chilled
	Port	Room temp.
	Muscatel	" "
	Tokay	" "
	Madeira	" "
	Marsala	" "
Coffee and After Dinner	Grappa	" "
	Cognac	" "
	Cointreau	" "
	Chartreuse	" "
	Crème de menthe	Frappéed
	Anisette	Room temp.
	Brandy	" "
	Maraschino	" "

CUSTOMS AND FESTIVALS

Capo d'Anno——*New Year's*

Since time immemorial, festivals and feasting have been associated in the mind of man with good fellowship, good food, and much rejoicing. New Year's at Nonni's was no exception. It was usually the gayest and most elaborate celebration of all the year.

The family's best silver was brought from safekeeping. All the large serving pieces were brilliantly polished, including the lovely old coffee set and silver decanter that were Nonni's special pride. Both had belonged to her mother and, year in, year out, always occupied the center of the alabaster top of the great walnut buffet against the side wall. Tall silver candelabra, filled with softly burning white candles, stood at either end of the buffet.

This piece of furniture was more than an elaborately carved decoration. In its several large drawers, linens were kept. Wine bottles and jugs were stored in the lower compartments. A smaller corner cabinet, in which Grandfather had ingeniously placed a wine barrel, always attracted attention. It was usually filled with a favorite vintage which was easily served by turning the old-fashioned wooden spigot which protruded from the decorated barrel head.

Two medium-sized serving tables stood near one end of the beautiful hand-carved dining table. The twelve matching chairs were made with rush-bottom seats. A newcomer might have wondered at two other pieces which completed the furnishings in the room. One was an enormous couch placed against the wall and the other was an ebony rocker which belonged to Grandfather. We of the family knew that he often rested there after eating. We had grown accustomed to his sitting in the rocker or even sinking into the soft Paisley cover and downy pillows of his couch. If he felt like it, why not? Didn't the ancient Romans have luxurious banquet couches?

Many Italian families celebrated New Year's Eve by serving an elaborate banquet shortly before midnight. But at Nonni's there was Asti Spumanti with a midnight supper. The real festivities took place on New Year's Day. It was the time when Nonni's dining room was transformed into a banquet hall with its doors swinging wide to welcome us to the feast. The large crystal chandeliers holding the oil lamps gleamed more brightly than ever. Perhaps it was because the lamps had been taken down to be trimmed and filled and the crystal washed and polished.

The whole house was astir and excited as the pungent aromas of specially prepared holiday food put our already expectant appetites on edge. We knew there would be the traditional *maialino arrostito* (roast suckling pig) served with crackling brown *carciofi arrostiti* (roasted artichokes. The dessert for that day was always one of Nonni's special *torta di ricotta* (Italian cheese pie) made still more delectable by the contrasting, bitter flavor of *caffe espresso.*

The adults exchanged gifts on New Year's and there was eating and merrymaking all day long. The dinner often lasted well into the night, and Nonni was showered with praise and blessings as family and departing friends shouted again: *"Buon Capo d'Anno* [*Happy New Year*]*!"*

Festa di San Giuseppe——————*St. Joseph's Day*

One of the early spring holidays with its correspondingly appropriate food and special holiday menu is the traditional St. Joseph's Day. It falls regularly on March 19. St. Joseph, the patron saint of home and family, is beloved by rich and poor alike. It is the tradition in Sicily for all wealthy families to prepare huge buffets laden with special meats, fish, pasta, fruits, vegetables, and desserts. Then all the less fortunate neighbors are invited to enjoy the feast.

The whole celebration begins with a religious tableau which has been rehearsed. Villagers have been selected to represent the Holy Family: an old man, a lovely young woman, and a little child. The three are seated at the head of the banquet table and remain there during the early part of the festivity. The village priest blesses the food, the "Holy Family" is served first by the host and hostess, and then it is officially "open house." The priest takes no other part in the celebration, nor does he eat any of the food especially prepared and provided for the guests.

All are free to come and go as they wish. The guests may eat what they choose and as much as pleases them. The festival lasts most of the day and well into the night. When all have been fed, they go on their way with thankful hearts and take the blessing of the host and hostess with them.

It is also customary for the village officials to arrange a public buffet in St. Joseph's honor. The banquet table invariably stands in the *piazza*—public square—opposite the doors of the cathedral. The table is usually built around two sides of the *piazza* in the form of a right angle. These village tables in the public squares may not be as elaborately decorated as those in the homes, but they sag beneath the weight of choice foods and wines contributed by the wealthy villagers. All come to this public table at some time during the day to pay homage to the great saint.

Many kinds of vegetable *minestras*—very thick soups—are prepared and served at this celebration, but no cheese is eaten on St. Joseph's Day. The spaghetti is not sprinkled with grated Incanestrato, but in its place a traditional mixture of toasted dry bread crumbs with fresh sardines and fennel sauce is used.

Lentils, *favas,* and all types of dried beans are cooked and served with escarole and other leafy vegetables—none of which is prepared with cheese.

Then there is the special dessert without which no St. Joseph's Day buffet could ever be called by that name. It is St. Joseph's Sfinge: a large round cream puff filled with ricotta (Italian cottage cheese) and topped with red cherries and sections of glazed orange.

Carnevale—*Carnival*

The festival known as *Carnevale* (Carnival) is the longest and gayest in the Italian calendar of annual celebrations. *Carnevale* continues the entire four weeks preceding Lent, but the latter part of the festival, called the "Two Days of the Shepherds," is the time when the whole family drops all activities to celebrate.

Food is served in great abundance and a traditional combination is *salsiccia con peperoni* (sausage with sautéed green peppers). The sausage is always broiled. Its extraordinary flavor comes from the blended seasonings of Caciocavallo cheese, chopped parsley, and fennel seed.

Everyone enters wholeheartedly into the fun of this merriest holiday of the year. There are music and dancing as young and old mingle in the public squares. Accordions, guitars, and mandolins supply the gay rhythms and lilting melodies of folk songs and ballads. Spontaneous shouts of merriment and laughter drift through the open doorways as the happy throngs of people fill the village streets.

Hilarious masquerades—similar to those of Mardi Gras—are held on the last night. At the stroke of midnight the church bells toll the beginning of Lent and all festivities cease for the forty days of fasting before Easter.

Pasqua—*Easter*

Even breakfast on Easter Day has its traditional menu. Eggs are prepared with vegetables and varied herbs. The choice and combination depend upon the particular taste of the family. Wine and *caffe espresso* complete the morning meal.

Dinner at Easter time is perhaps the most festive one of all the year. Holiday bread, baked in many different shapes and designs, is prepared for children and grownups alike. The yellow dough is molded into dolls, baskets, and bunnies. In the center of each basket a gaily colored egg may be lodged and sometimes one is hidden under the arm of a little doll. Each member of the family is certain to receive a piece of holiday bread baked in his or her favorite design. Often Nonni used to bake a huge ring of festive bread and surround it completely with at least a dozen or more colored eggs. This decorative bread ring was placed on the Easter table as the center decoration.

Many other favorites were also prepared for us on that day. We used to have great fun watching Nonni roast the traditional *agnellino* (baby lamb). And no Easter dinner was complete without artichokes roasted to a golden brown.

For dessert there was always a great variety of cookies and nuts with spumoni. The dessert served most frequently was the one associated with the day as traditional: the tempting *cassatelli* (cream tartlets). Finally a large basket of piping-hot roasted chestnuts was placed before us; despite our satisfied feeling, we relished them with much gusto.

To give you an idea of what Nonni's Easter menu really looked like, had she written it down for you, it has been included in the list of festival menus.

Natale—*Christmas*

Christmas Eve is ushered in with quiet solemnity and there is a traditional supper, usually served late in the evening before the family attends midnight Mass. No meat is ever eaten on that Holy Night, but in its place fish is always served. In many households it has become the custom to eat only *capitone,* a species of large thick eels. This meal is not an elaborate one and it has an air of solemn festivity. Traditional foods are included in the menu, and the soup is usually chicken broth for which *cappelletti* (little hats) have been freshly prepared. The dessert is always a rich, decorative *cassata* (cream tart).

On Christmas Day, when the children exchange gifts, there is much joy and festivity. A regular holiday feast is prepared for which each family makes up its own menu of special favorites. Invariably there are two or three rich desserts: one of these is certain to be the traditional, decorative and honeyed *pignolata-strufoli* (pine-nut clusters).

In Nonni's home at Christmas time there was always an extra-large *pignolata* placed on the buffet as an effective centerpiece. It was a great favorite with her, and for practically every celebration Nonni would also include a *cassata.* More sweets were served at Christmas than at any other time during the year, and there were *amaretti* (macaroons) and *pallottole d'aranci* (orange balls) for the children to munch as they played with their new toys.

All holidays remind us of the gay celebrations we enjoyed with Nonni. No matter where we are, when there is good food and merry music in the joyous gatherings of our family and friends, those times are forever associated in our minds and hearts with the traditions given to all of us by our loving Nonni.

CHAPTER THREE

Festival Menus

IN CHAPTER TWO, "WINES, CUSTOMS, AND FESTIVALS," WE told how most Italian holidays are occasions for gay celebrations. Naturally, menus for such days can be very unusual and highly individual.

Nonni's special menus were so characteristically hers that several complete ones are given here.

BIRTHDAY MENU — COMPLEANNO

Chilled Sherry or Cocktail
Antipasto
Rice Milanese
Broiled Italian Sausage
Chicken with Orégano
Broccoli with Olives
Escarole Salad
Cream Cake de Luxe
Fruit
Nuts
Caffe Espresso
Cointreau

Chilled claret or burgundy may be served with this dinner. Well-chilled champagne with Cream Cake.

CARNIVAL MENU — CARNEVALE

Cocktails
Antipasto
Gnocchi with Plain Tomato Sauce
Broiled Holiday Sausage
Sautéed Green Peppers
Orange and Lemon Salad
Torta di Pistacchio
Fruit
Caffe Espresso
Liqueur

Burgundy may be served during entire meal.

CHRISTENING MENU — BATTESIMO

Cocktails
Antipasto
Macaroni with Mushroom Sauce
Veal Rollettes
Roasted Suckling Pig
Steamed Escarole
Roasted Peppers
Lemon and Orange Salad
Amaretti
Spumoni
Assorted Nuts
Caffe Espresso
Champagne
Maraschino

Chilled burgundy may be served with the antipasto and roast. Champagne with dessert. Maraschino with coffee.

CONFIRMATION MENU CRESIMA

Cocktails
Antipasto
Noodle Soup
Buttered Spring Chicken
Pan-Browned Potatoes
Broiled Mushrooms
Mixed Salad
Aunt Lena's Anise Slices
Spumoni
Mixed Nuts
Caffe Espresso
Brandy and Benedictine

Chilled claret may be served with chicken. Room temperature muscatel with the dessert.

CHRISMAS EVE SUPPER MENU VIGILIA DI NATALE

Vermouth with Lemon Peel
Antipasto
Cappelletti in Broth
Capitone
String Bean Salad
Finocchio
Cassata
Fresh Figs—Prickly Pears
Roasted Chestnuts
Caffe Espresso
Maraschino or Benedictine

Meat is never served on Christmas Eve. Serve sauterne with broth and *capitone*.
Port or tokay with *cassata*.

CHRISMAS DAY MENU NATALE

Chilled Marsala
Antipasto
Chicken Broth
Lasagne Imbottite
Italian Sausage
Roast Chicken
Fried Eggplant
Finocchio Salad
Pignolata
Assorted Nuts
Fruit
Caffe Espresso
Brandy

Burgundy may be served during dinner. Port or sweet sherry with *pignolata.*

NEW YEAR'S EVE NOTTE DI CAPO D'ANNO

Chilled Vermouth with Lemon Peel
Mafalde with Meat Sauce
Chicken with Mushrooms
Roasted Green Peppers
Tomato Salad with Orégano Dressing
Zabaglione
Fruit
Caffe Espresso
Champagne

Well-chilled chablis may be served with chicken.

NEW YEAR'S MENU CAPO D'ANNO

Chilled Sherry
Antipasto
Macaroni with Plain Tomato Sauce
Roast Suckling Pig
Boiled Artichokes with Salad Dressing
Escarole Salad—Finocchio
Torta di Ricotta
Toasted Almonds
Fruit
Caffe Espresso
Anisette or Cognac
Asti Spumanti

Claret or burgundy may be served with dinner.
Port, muscatel, or champagne with dessert.

TYPICAL ST. JOSEPH'S BUFFET FESTA DI SAN GIUSEPPE

Chilled Marsala
Lentil Soup
Spaghetti with Finocchio and Sardine Sauce
Roasted Artichokes
Italian Sausage
Escarole Salad
St. Joseph's Sfinge
Amaretti—Macaroons
Roasted Nuts—Green Almonds—Fruit
Caffe Espresso
Benedictine or Anisette

During the entire repast, a rather tart red wine is served, although a sweeter one may be used if preferred.

EASTER MENU PASQUA

Chilled Marsala
Manicotti with Tomato Sauce
Whole Roasted Baby Lamb
Sautéed Spinach
Roasted Artichokes
Mixed Salad
Roasted Chestnuts
Cassatelli
Fruit in Season
Asti Spumanti
Caffe Espresso
Cognac

Chilled claret or riesling may be served with baby lamb.

SPRINGTIME MENU PRIMAVERA

Vermouth with Lemon Peel
Antipasto
Chicken Broth with Pastina
Veal with Marsala
Sautéed Broccoli
Dandelion Salad
Bel Paese Cheese with Toasted Crackers
Fruit in Season
Caffe Espresso
Anisette

Well-chilled light dry sauterne or riesling may be served with veal.

SUMMER MENU ESTATE

Old Sherry
Spaghetti with Clam Sauce
Asparagus Parmesan
Chicken with Orégano
Romaine Salad
Stuffed Peaches
Aunt Lena's Anise Slices
Spumoni
Caffe Espresso

Chilled claret may be served with spaghetti. A light dry sauterne or chablis with chicken.

AUTUMN MENU AUTUNNO

Chilled Marsala
Antipasto
Minestrone
Brandied Duck
Stuffed Mushrooms
Cucumber and Tomato Salad
Apple with Gorgonzola Cheese
Nuts
Caffe Espresso
Cognac

Chilled burgundy or bordeaux may be served with duck.

WINTER MENU INVERNO

Vermouth or Cocktail
Antipasto
Ravioli with Plain Tomato Sauce
Beef à la Mode
Fried Eggplant
Roasted Artichokes
Mixed Salad
Zabaglione
Fruit in Season
Caffe Espresso
Benedictine

Chilled burgundy or zinfandel may be served with ravioli and beef.

ANY SPECIAL WINTER HOLIDAY MENU FESTE INVERNALE

Chilled Marsala
Antipasto
Cappelletti in Chicken Broth
Roasted Pheasant
Rabbit Stew
Sautéed Mushrooms
Rice Croquettes
Mixed Salad
Assorted Cheeses
Gorgonzola, Bel Paese, Strachino, and Scamozza
Zuppa Inglese
Caffe Espresso
Cognac—Chartreuse

Burgundy may be served with dinner. Cognac or chartreuse with caffe espresso.

WEDDING MENU SPOSALIZIO

Cocktails
Chicken Broth
Stuffed Noodles
Roasted Whole Baby Lamb
Roasted Artichokes
Mushrooms Parmesan
Chicory Salad
Cassata
Fruit in Season
Cheese
Caffe Espresso
Brandy
Chartreuse

Well-chilled sauterne may be served with chicken broth.
Chianti with stuffed noodles and lamb.
Champagne with the dessert.

CHAPTER FOUR

Salute!

DINNER BEGINS WITH ANTIPASTO

THE GLASS IS RAISED; THE TOAST IS GIVEN—*"Salute!"* (sa-looh-tay). Dinner begins with antipasto—the Italian appetizer.

The combinations served can be of individual choice, and the preparation of an attractive antipasto plate calls for much ingenuity. Its color and taste appeal depend on the variety of appetizers used as well as the manner in which they are arranged. For instance, lettuce and *finocchio* (a species of Italian celery) used as a green-and-white border will improve the appearance of even a usual selection of celery, radishes, pickled beets, salami, and *acciughe* (anchovies). If a still more colorful combination is preferred, simply add one or two large *olive nere all'olio* (Italian black olives in oil) and a strip of brilliant pimiento.

Another typical Italian variation would include *funghi con aceto e olio* (sautéed mushrooms in vinegar and oil), sliced hard-boiled eggs, *uovo di tonno* (tuna-fish roe), lettuce, and wafer-thin slices of *prosciutto* (Italian ham).

Still another appetizing combination would be *peperoncini all'aceto* (small green pickled peppers), two or three *carciofini* (artichoke hearts), a pimiento, a stalk of *finocchio, salsiccia secca* (dry pork sausage) sliced thinly, and *acciughe.*

When the choice has been made and the plate prepared, it is customary to pour olive oil and a small quantity of wine vinegar over the combination.

As one becomes familiar with antipasto one will find it fun to make up combinations to include the favorite delicacies of each individual. For instance:

Lettuce and Sliced Tomatoes
Anchovies
Quartered Hard-boiled Eggs
Radishes
Salami
Celery and Ripe Olives

OR

Lettuce and Pickled Beets
Prosciutto (Italian Ham)
Radishes
Celery Hearts
Herring Roe
Green Olives

OR

Carciofini (Artichoke Hearts)
Capocollo (Sliced Smoked Pork)
Lettuce and Finocchio
Sliced Tomatoes
Quartered Hard-boiled Eggs
Peperoncini all'Aceto
Ripe Olives

Usually, in most Italian households, a small glass of slightly chilled vermouth with a twist of lemon peel is served with this course. Sherry is also good if preferred.

Many of the antipasto mentioned may be purchased in Italian stores and delicatessens.

ANTIPASTO LIST

ACCIUGHE: Anchovy filets.

CAPOCOLLO: Delicately smoked pork, sliced very thin as a salami.

CARCIOFINI: Artichoke hearts.

FINOCCHIO: An anise-flavored species of celery with

a lacy green leaf at top. Also served after dinner or in salads.

FUNGHI CON ACETO E OLIO: Sautéed cold mushrooms, marinated in Italian or French dressing.

OLIVE: Olives—green or black.

OLIVE NERE ALL'OLIO: Black olives cured in oil instead of brine.

PEPERONCINI ALL'ACETO: Small green peppers pickled in vinegar—of very tart flavor—they take the place of the American sour pickle.

PIMIENTO: Sweet red peppers.

PROSCIUTTO: Slightly pungent smoky-flavored Italian ham, served in wafer-thin slices as is salami.

RADICI: Radishes.

SALAMI: Highly seasoned Italian sausage, served in wafer-thin slices.

SALSICCIA SECCA: Very dry pork sausage, served in wafer-thin slices as is salami.

SALSICCIA SECCA CON PEPERONI: Very peppery dry sausage, served in wafer-thin slices.

SEDANI: Celery hearts.

UOVO DI ARINGHE: Herring roe.

UOVO DI TONNO: Tuna-fish roe.

Recipes

CHAPTER FIVE

Soups

Fish Soups

BRODO DI PESCE CON TAGLIARINI

FISH BROTH WITH NARROW NOODLES

2½ lbs. whiting
¼ lb. tagliarini (narrow noodles)
1 large onion, sliced
1 large carrot, chopped
2 large fresh tomatoes, chopped
3 stalks celery
2 tbs. butter
2 tbs. olive oil
½ cup grated Parmesan cheese
2 qts. boiling water
Salt and pepper to taste

Have fish cleaned; leave whole; melt butter in large deep saucepan or pot; add olive oil; heat; add onion, carrot, and celery; cook over medium flame for 10 minutes; add tomatoes, salt and pepper to taste; add rapidly boiling water; cover. Cook slowly for 30 minutes. Add fish; boil slowly for 15 minutes. Remove fish carefully, using a spatula to prevent breaking. Set aside; keep hot by placing platter over steaming water.

Strain broth through colander. Bring to a boil; add tagliarini (noodles); cook 12 minutes or until tender. Serve broth very hot and sprinkle generously with grated Parmesan.

Serve fish separately with green salad and lemon slices. Serves 4 to 6.

Meat Soups

BRODO DI MANZO

BEEF BROTH

2 lbs. shank beef
1 shank bone with marrow
3 springs parsley
1 ripe tomato
1 carrot
1 onion
1 potato
6 qts. water
Salt and pepper to taste

Put all ingredients in cold water. Bring to a boil. Lower flame and cook slowly for 2 hours in covered pot.

Remove meat and bone. Remove marrow from bone; add marrow to broth. Strain broth and vegetables through colander or sieve.

Use as basic beef broth or stock.

MINESTRONE MILANESE

MINESTRONE MILAN STYLE

½ cup kidney beans
½ cup rice
¼ cup olive oil
1 No. 2 can tomatoes
1 clove garlic
2 cups chopped spinach
Pinch of sage
Salt and pepper to taste
2 qts. prepared soup stock
1 sliced onion
1 tbs. chopped parsley
2 stalks celery, diced
2 cups shredded cabbage
2 cups chopped carrots
¼ cup grated Parmesan cheese

Soak beans overnight. Drain.

In large pot, sauté, in hot oil, garlic, onion, and fresh vegetables for ten minutes. Stir. Add rice, beans, salt and pepper, and soup stock. Cover. Simmer until beans and rice are tender and most of soup has been absorbed.

This usually takes about 1½ hours. Add cheese and mix thoroughly.

Produces a thick, nourishing soup. Serves 6 to 8.

NONNI'S ZUPPA DI POLLO

NONNI'S CHICKEN SOUP

1 plump fowl (4-5 lbs.)
2 large carrots
1 large onion
3 stalks celery
1 large fresh tomato
3 springs parsley
Salt and pepper to taste

Place all ingredients in 6 quarts of cold water. Bring to a boil. Lower flame and simmer for 2 hours or until fowl is thoroughly tender and meat falls from bone. Remove fowl from pot. Strain all vegetables through a sieve. Heat exact amount for serving.

Serve piping hot and clear. Serves 8.

ZUPPA VEGETALE CON POLPETTINI

VEGETABLE SOUP WITH MEAT BALLS

5 qts. water
2 lbs. lean beef
1 veal or beef bone
2 large onions, halved
2 stalks celery
3 carrots
1 No. 2 can tomatoes
3 sprigs parsley
Salt and pepper to taste

Cook all these ingredients in large covered pot over low flame for 2 hours.

Strain, then add:

2 diced carrots
2 diced potatoes
3 tbs. rice
1 cup fresh peas
*1½ dozen small meat balls**

Boil slowly for 30 minutes in covered pot. Serve very hot. (If desired, sprinkle with grated Parmesan cheese.)

* Prepare recipe as for Polpetti (meat balls).

ZUPPA DI SPINACI E RISO

SPINACH SOUP WITH RICE

4 qts. water
2 lbs. lean beef
1 veal or beef bone
1 large onion, halved
1 tsp. chopped parsley
2 cups boiled rice
2 cups cooked chopped fresh spinach
3 stalks celery, diced
1 No. 2 can tomatoes
3 diced carrots
2 tbs. olive oil
½ cup grated Parmesan cheese
Salt and pepper to taste

Place all ingredients except cheese, olive oil, rice, and spinach in a large pot. Cover. Cook for 2 hours over low flame.

Strain broth and vegetables.

Sauté spinach in olive oil for 2 minutes; add rice and mix. Add this mixture to broth and strained vegetables; cook 3 minutes. Serve hot with grated Parmesan cheese for added flavor. Serves 6 to 8.

Beef used for soup may be cut into small cubes when cold; add sliced onion, parsley, a little olive oil, and vinegar to taste; toss and serve with mixed green salad. Sliced tomatoes may also be placed around dish to add color and flavor.

Vegetable Soups

ZUPPA DI LENTICCHI #1

LENTIL SOUP #1

1 lb. lentils
3 qts. water
1 chopped onion
2 tbs. butter
2 tbs. olive oil
Salt and pepper to taste

Wash lentils. Place in pot with cold water. Cook over medium flame about 1½ hours or until lentils are soft. Add salt and pepper.

Melt butter in separate saucepan; add oil; sauté onion for about 5 minutes or until soft and slightly brown.

When lentils are done, strain soup through sieve or colander; add onion and oil mixture; stir thoroughly. This produces a thick soup. Keep hot over low flame until served. Serve very hot. Sprinkle with grated Parmesan cheese if desired.

Serves 4 to 6.

ZUPPA DI LENTICCHI #2

LENTIL SOUP #2

½ lb. lentils
1 onion
1 clove garlic
2 stalks celery
4 tbs. olive oil
1 tsp. chopped parsley
½ cup tomatoes (stewed or canned)
Salt and pepper to taste

Cook lentils in 2 quarts of boiling salted water for 1 hour. Chop onion, garlic, and celery; put into saucepan with oil and parsley; cook until slightly browned; add tomatoes and cook for 10 minutes longer. Pour this mixture into pot with lentils; cover; let simmer for 15 minutes or until lentils are soft.

Serve in deep soup bowls and sprinkle with grated Romano cheese if desired. Serves 4.

MINESTRONE DI ZIO GIUSEPPE

UNCLE JOE'S MINESTRONE

1 lb. fresh peas
1 cup diced celery
2 diced carrots
1 large onion, sliced
1 cup canned tomatoes
½ cup olive oil
¾ lbs. vermicelli
3 qts. water
½ cup grated Romano cheese
3 diced potatoes
Salt and pepper to taste

Clean all vegetables. In saucepan, sauté onions and potatoes in hot olive oil about 10 minutes or until medium brown. Add tomatoes, salt and pepper; cover; cook slowly about 15 minutes.

In separate pot, bring 3 quarts of water to boiling point. Add celery, peas, and carrots; cover; cook about 15 minutes or until tender. Add all sautéed vegetables and vermicelli broken into 1-inch pieces; cover; cook 20 minutes.

Serve very hot with grated Romano cheese. Serves 6 to 8.

MINESTRONE SEMPLICE

PLAIN MINESTRONE

½ lb. ditalini†
1 chopped onion
2 tbs. olive oil
2 cups string beans cut into small pieces
1 tsp. chopped parsley
3 qts. boiling water
2 ozs. grated Parmesan cheese
3 tbs. butter
3 stalks celery, diced
2 large potatoes, diced
1 cup fresh peas
Salt and pepper to taste

Cook onion in oil and butter about 3 minutes or until slightly brown; add celery, potatoes; cook for 10 minutes in covered pot. Add 3 quarts boiling water; cook 15 minutes more. Add string beans, peas, ditalini, salt and pepper; cover; cook slowly another 20 minutes.

Serve very hot. Sprinkle with parsley and cheese. Serves 6 to 8.

MINESTRA DI PASTA E FAGIOLI

PASTA AND KIDNEY BEAN SOUP

1 lb. kidney beans
½ cup chopped celery
1 large onion, minced
1 clove garlic
6 tbs. olive oil
1 chopped carrot
1 No. 2 can tomatoes
½ lb. tubettina (pasta)
½ cup grated Romano cheese
Salt and pepper to taste

† Ditalini: pasta; very short tubular type.

Soak beans overnight. Drain.

Cook beans in 3 quarts of salted boiling water in covered pot for 1 hour. Add all other ingredients except tubettini and olive oil. Cook slowly for 1 hour.

Cook tubettini in 3 quarts of rapidly boiling salted water about 10 minutes. Drain; add to beans and vegetables. Add olive oil; simmer about 15 minutes.

Serve very hot. Sprinkle with grated Romano cheese. Serves 6.

MINESTRA DI ZIA TERESA

AUNT TESSIE'S MINESTRA

1 lb. kidney beans
3 bunches celery
1 clove garlic, chopped
1 tsp. orégano
4 tbs. olive oil
4 qts. water
1 large onion, sliced
4 tbs. grated Romano cheese
Salt and pepper to taste

Scrub and dice celery. Wash beans.

Place beans, celery, garlic, and onion in cold water; bring to a boil. Cover; simmer over very low flame about 1½ hours or until beans and celery are soft. Add oil, orégano, salt and pepper to taste. Simmer 15 minutes.

Serve very hot. Serves 4 to 6.

CHAPTER SIX

Spaghetti and Pasta

CAPPELLETTI

LITTLE HATS

Stuffing:

1 lb. ricotta (Italian cottage cheese)
1 chicken breast
2 tbs. butter
1 whole egg
1 egg yolk
Pinch of nutmeg
Pinch of salt and pepper
3 tbs. grated Parmesan cheese

Stuffing: Brown chicken breast in butter; add salt and pepper to taste; chop very fine. Add it to other stuffing ingredients; mix thoroughly.

Pasta: (Dough)

1 lb. flour
3 eggs
1 cup lukewarm water
Pinch of salt
1 tbs. butter

Pasta: Place flour on board; beat eggs slightly; stir eggs into flour; add butter; gradually add enough water to form firm dough. Knead well until smooth and manageable. Cut in half; roll with rolling pin into thin sheets on lightly floured board. Cut into disks with a biscuit cutter; place 1 teaspoon stuffing on center of each disk; fold one side over to form the little hat. Press edges gently but firmly to prevent filling from falling out.

When all ingredients are used, drop the cappelletti into 6 quarts of rapidly boiling salted water; cook about 5 minutes or until dough is tender. Drain; put on hot platter; serve with plain tomato sauce and grated Parmesan cheese.

Cappelletti may also be boiled in chicken broth and served as soup.

CONCHIGLIE E PATATE

SEA SHELLS AND POTATOES

¾ lb. conchiglie (pasta)
1½ lbs. potatoes
2 sliced onions
1 No. 2 can tomatoes
4 tbs. olive oil
2 tbs. chopped parsley
½ cup grated Pecorino cheese
Salt and pepper to taste

Peel and dice potatoes. Heat oil in large saucepan; add potatoes and onions. Cook 10 minutes; stir constantly to prevent burning. Add tomatoes, salt, pepper, and parsley; cover; cook over low flame for 30 minutes.

Cook conchiglie in 3 quarts of rapidly boiling salted water 20 minutes or until tender. Drain; place in large hot bowl; add hot sauce, potatoes, and cheese. Mix thoroughly.

Serve very hot. Serves 4 to 6.

FUSILLI CON CAVOLFIORE

FUSILLI WITH CAULIFLOWER

1 lb. fusilli (pasta)
1 small cauliflower
1 large diced onion
1 No. 2 can tomatoes
4 tbs. olive oil
1 tbs. pignoli (pine nuts)
1 tbs. currants
3 filets of anchovy
Salt and pepper to taste

Wash and break or cut cauliflower into small pieces. Cook in rapidly boiling salted water about 12 minutes or until tender but not soft. Drain; set aside.

Heat oil in saucepan; add onion; cook 3 minutes or until soft. Cut up anchovies; add; stir about 2 minutes or until dissolved. Add tomatoes; cover; simmer 20 minutes. Add cauliflower, pine nuts, currants, and very little salt and pepper. Mix well; keep hot over very low flame.

Cook fusilli in 4 quarts of rapidly boiling salted water 15 minutes or until tender. Drain; place in hot bowl; add cauliflower and sauce.

Serve very hot in individual plates. Serves 4 to 6. (If desired, Fusilli with Cauliflower may be sprinkled with grated Romano cheese just before serving.)

GNOCCHI

DUMPLINGS

4 lbs. potatoes
5 cups flour
Salt to taste

Boil and rice potatoes. Gradually add 5 cups of flour. Knead until a smooth manageable dough is obtained. If necessary, add a little more flour.

Roll dough into long ropelike strips about ¾ inch thick; cut into ¾-inch pieces; dip in flour. Use prong of fork to make dented design on each piece.

Boil in 8 quarts of rapidly boiling salted water for about 10 minutes. Drain. Place on large platter or individual plates.

Serve with tomato sauce and sprinkle with grated Parmesan cheese. Serves 6 to 8.

LASAGNE IMBOTTITE

STUFFED NOODLES

Sauce:

1 large can plum tomatoes
½ can tomato paste
½ cup hot water
4 tbs. olive oil
2 cloves garlic
1 stalk celery, diced
Salt and pepper to taste

Stuffing:

1½ lbs. ricotta (Italian cottage cheese)
¾ lb. sausage
1½ lbs. broad noodles
1½ cups cubed Mozzarella
1½ cups grated Parmesan cheese
Salt and pepper to taste

Blend tomato paste with hot water. Brown garlic in hot olive oil about 3 minutes; add celery, blended tomato paste and plum tomatoes; boil over high flame for 3 minutes; lower flame; cover; simmer for one hour. Add pepper and salt.

Broil sausage under high flame about 15 minutes or until brown on both sides; cut into small pieces.

Cook noodles in rapidly boiling salted water about 15 minutes or until tender, but not too soft. Drain.

Pour ½ cup sauce into bottom of baking pan; over this place layer of noodles, than layer of grated Parmesan cheese, a layer of sauce, a layer of Mozzarella, sausage, and a tablespoon of ricotta here and there. Repeat this process in layers until all ingredients are used. Top layer should be sauce and grated cheese. Bake in moderate oven for 15 minutes or until firm. When done, the Lasagne Imbottite is cut into serving portions. Place on individual plates; top with more sauce and grated cheese.

Serve very hot. Serves 8 to 10.

LASAGNE AL FORNO

BAKED NOODLES

1 lb. noodles (½ in. wide)
1 small Mozzarella (¾ lb.)
½ cup grated Parmesan cheese
4 tbs. olive oil
1 large chopped onion
1 large can tomato purée
½ tsp. sugar
Salt and pepper to taste

Brown onion in oil; add tomatoes, salt, pepper, and sugar. Cook slowly in covered pan for one hour; stir frequently.

Cook noodles about 15 minutes or until tender (stirring constantly to prevent sticking) in 5 quarts of rapidly boiling salted water. Drain. Alternate in baking dish layers of noodles, sauce, thin slices of Mozzarella, and a sprinkling of grated Parmesan cheese. Continue this process until all ingredients are used. Bake in moderate oven 15 minutes.

Serve very hot in individual dishes; top with more sauce and grated Parmesan cheese. Serves 4 to 6.

MANICOTTI

MACARONI MUFFS

Pasta: (Dough)

1 lb. flour
1 cup lukewarm water
½ tsp. salt
3 eggs
1 tbs. butter

Stuffing:

1 lb. ricotta (Italian cottage cheese)
¼ lb. chopped ham
2 eggs
½ cup grated Romano cheese
Salt and pepper to taste

Prepare plain Tomato Sauce #1.

Pasta: Mix flour, butter, 3 eggs, and salt. Gradually add enough water to make a medium-soft dough. Knead into a smooth ball. Cut into two sections and roll on lightly floured board until thin (the usual noodle thinness). Cut into rectangles, 5 by 6 inches.

Stuffing: Mix ricotta and eggs; add chopped ham. Use very little salt and pepper; keep mixing until well blended.

Spread 1½ tablespoons of mixture on each piece of dough; roll and close; moisten edges and press tightly to prevent filling from falling out. These are the little manicotti.

Cook manicotti about 10 minutes in extra-large pot of boiling salted water (about 8 quarts). When dough is tender, drain carefully with flat skimmer.

Place several manicotti on individual plates; cover manicotti with tomato sauce and a layer of grated Romano cheese.

Serve very hot. Serves 6 to 8.

PASTA CON RICOTTA

MACARONI WITH RICOTTA

1 lb. any type cut macaroni
1 lb. ricotta (Italian cottage cheese)
½ cup milk
2 ozs. butter
½ cup Parmesan cheese (grated)
Salt to taste

Cook macaroni about 15 minutes or until tender in 5 quarts of rapidly boiling salted water. Drain; put back in pot; add butter.

Mix ricotta with milk in a bowl until smooth. Pour over hot macaroni; simmer 3 minutes over low flame in covered pot. Sprinkle with grated Parmesan cheese.

Serve very hot. Serves 4 to 6.

RAVIOLI

Pasta: (Dough)

3 cups flour
2 eggs
2 tbs. butter
1 cup warm water
¼ tsp. salt

Filling:

1 cup minced cooked chicken
1 cup chopped cooked spinach
½ cup bread crumbs
⅓ cup grated Parmesan cheese
2 eggs
2 tsp. chopped parsley
½ clove garlic, chopped
Salt and pepper to taste

Pasta: Sift flour and salt together. Place on a board; drop eggs in center; add butter; mix. Gradually add enough water to make a rather stiff dough. Knead until smooth; cover and let stand about 10 minutes. Cut in half; roll on lightly floured board until very thin.

Filling: Beat eggs lightly. Blend all other ingredients; gradually add enough beaten egg to hold firmly together. Drop teaspoonfuls of filling about 2 inches apart on one sheet of dough until filling is used. Then cover with other sheet. With finger tips gently press around each mound of filling to form a little filled square. Cut squares apart with pastry cutter. Place 8 quarts of salted water in deep pot. When rapidly boiling, cook ravioli about 10 minutes or until dough is tender. Remove carefully with perforated soup skimmer; place serving portions on individual heated plates; top with Plain Tomato Sauce; sprinkle with grated Parmesan cheese.

Serve very hot. Serves 6.

RIGATONI CON SALSICCIA

RIGATONI WITH SAUSAGE

1 lb. rigatoni (pasta)
1 lb. Italian pork sausage
3 tbs. olive oil
1 chopped onion
1 lb. fresh mushrooms
1 bay leaf
1 large can tomato purée
½ cup grated Pecorino cheese
1 clove garlic
Salt and pepper to taste

Cut sausage in 1-inch pieces; place in hot skillet with olive oil; brown slightly for about 10 minutes. Add onion, mushrooms (well cleaned and sliced), garlic, salt, and pepper; simmer for 15 minutes. Add tomato purée and bay leaf. Cover pan; cook slowly for 1 hour. Remove bay leaf.

Cook rigatoni about 20 minutes in 5 quarts of rapidly boiling salted water. When tender, drain and place in baking dish. Add sausage and sauce. Mix. Sprinkle with grated Pecorino cheese. Bake in moderate oven about 10 minutes.

Serve very hot. Serves 6.

SPAGHETTI CON ACCIUGHE

SPAGHETTI WITH ANCHOVIES

1 lb. spaghetti
½ cup olive oil
1 clove garlic
12 filets of anchovy
½ cup grated Parmesan cheese
Salt and pepper to taste

Fry garlic in hot oil about 3 minutes or until brown. Then remove garlic. Cut anchovies in ½-inch pieces and add to hot oil; cook for 2 minutes; stir constantly. Add a little pepper.

Cook spaghetti about 20 minutes or until tender in rapidly boiling salted water. Drain; arrange on individual heated plates. Pour sauce over spaghetti. Top with grated Parmesan cheese. Use salt very sparingly since anchovies are very salty. Serves 4 to 6.

SPAGHETTI AL BURRO

SPAGHETTI WITH BUTTER

1 lb. spaghetti
¼ lb. butter
2 ozs. grated Parmesan cheese
Salt to taste

Cook spaghetti in 5 quarts of rapidly boiling salted water for 20 minutes. Drain. Melt butter in saucepan over low flame. Serve spaghetti in heated individual plates. Pour melted butter over steaming spaghetti; sprinkle with grated Parmesan cheese.

Serve immediately. Serves 4 to 6.

SPAGHETTI E FINOCCHIO SICILIANA

SPAGHETTI WITH FENNEL SICILIAN

1 lb. spaghetti
1 lb. thin fresh finocchio
4 tbs. olive oil
1 chopped onion
1 cup cold water
1 lb. fresh sardines
1½ cups toasted bread crumbs
1 tbs. pine nuts
1 tbs. seedless raisins
Salt and pepper to taste

Clean and bone sardines.

Clean finocchio. Cook in 1 quart of boiling salted water

about 15 minutes or until tender. Drain; cut into half-inch pieces.

Cook onion in olive oil, in saucepan, about 3 minutes or until golden brown; add sardines; sauté 10 minutes, stirring frequently to prevent burning; add finocchio, raisins, and pine nuts; add cup of cold water, salt and pepper; simmer slowly for about 10 minutes. The fish may break up during this process.

Cook spaghetti about 20 minutes in 5 quarts of rapidly boiling salted water. Drain; put in deep dish; add half of finocchio mixture to the spaghetti; sprinkle with half of toasted bread crumbs. Mix. Serve on individual plates. Top with bread crumbs and more finocchio mixture. No cheese is used.

Serve very hot. Serves 6. This is a traditional St. Joseph's Day dish.

SPAGHETTI CON SALSA DI CARNE

SPAGHETTI WITH MEAT SAUCE

1 lb. spaghetti
½ clove garlic
½ lb. chopped beef
1 chopped onion
2 tsp. chopped parsley
1 large can plum tomatoes
½ cup grated Pecorino cheese
4 tbs. olive oil
½ cup chopped mushrooms
Salt and pepper to taste

Fry chopped beef in hot oil about 10 minutes or until slightly brown. Add garlic, onion, mushrooms, and parsley; sauté for 10 minutes. Stir occasionally. Add salt, pepper, and tomatoes; simmer 1 hour or until sauce is of thick consistency.

Cook spaghetti 20 minutes in 5 quarts of rapidly boiling salted water. Drain. Place on heated serving dish; add hot sauce; sprinkle with grated Pecorino cheese. Any type macaroni may be served with this meat sauce.

Serves 4 to 6.

SPAGHETTI MARINARA

SPAGHETTI WITH MARINER SAUCE

1 lb. spaghetti
1 large can plum tomatoes
4 tbs. olive oil
2 sliced onions
1 clove garlic
2 ozs. grated Romano cheese
¼ tsp. orégano
¼ tsp. sugar
2 filets of anchovy
Salt and pepper to taste

Sauté onion and garlic in hot oil about 5 minutes or until soft; remove garlic; add tomatoes; cook rapidly for 5 minutes; then lower flame and simmer for 1 hour. Add anchovies cut into small pieces. Use very little salt and pepper; add sugar. Cook slowly for 10 minutes. Add orégano; stir. Keep hot over low flame until ready to serve.

Cook spaghetti as usual. Drain; arrange on hot platter and pour sauce over spaghetti. Sprinkle with grated cheese.

Serves 4 to 6.

SPAGHETTI CON MELENZANI

SPAGHETTI WITH EGGPLANT

1 lb. spaghetti
1 large eggplant
1 large can plum tomatoes
1 clove garlic
1 tbs. chopped parsley
1 minced onion
2 ozs. grated Parmesan cheese
4 tbs. olive oil
½ cup peanut oil
Salt and pepper to taste

Place olive oil in saucepan; add onion, garlic, and parsley; cook 3 minutes. Add tomatoes, salt and pepper; simmer slowly for 1 hour. Stir frequently.

Meanwhile, peel eggplant; slice it lengthwise about ½ inch thick; sprinkle a little salt on each slice; put in colander and allow to drain for 15 minutes. Then rinse in cold water; pat dry with absorbent paper. Fry slices in hot peanut oil about 3 minutes on each side or until light brown and soft. When done, set eggplant aside and keep hot.

Cook spaghetti as usual. Drain; place on hot platter and

pour tomato sauce over spaghetti. Cut eggplant slices in half or in thin strips; arrange over tomato sauce and sprinkle generously with grated Parmesan cheese.

Serve hot. Serves 4 to 6.

SPAGHETTI CON SALSA SEMPLICE DI POMODORO

SPAGHETTI WITH PLAIN TOMATO SAUCE

1 large can tomato purée
2 cloves garlic
4 tbs. olive oil
1 bay leaf
1 lb. spaghetti
2 ozs. grated Romano cheese
½ tsp. sugar
Salt and pepper to taste

Heat olive oil in saucepan; add garlic and brown for 2 minutes; add tomato purée, sugar, bay leaf, salt and pepper. Cook over low flame for 1 hour. Stir frequently to prevent burning. Then remove bay leaf and garlic.

Cook spaghetti about 20 minutes or until tender, in rapidly boiling salted water. Drain; place on heated platter.

Pour sauce over spaghetti; sprinkle generously with grated Romano cheese.

Serve very hot. Serves 4 to 6.

SPAGHETTI CON SALSA DI VONGOLI

SPAGHETTI WITH CLAM SAUCE

See recipe for Clam Sauce

Boil one pound of spaghetti or other type macaroni for about 15 minutes in 5 quarts of rapidly boiling salted water. It will be *al dente,* which means medium. Or cook until soft, if you prefer it that way.

Drain; arrange on heated platter or individual serving dishes and pour very hot Clam Sauce over it.

This appetizing dish may be served with or without grated Romano cheese.

Serves 4 to 6.

SPAGHETTINI BAGARIA

THIN SPAGHETTI BAGARIA STYLE

1 lb. spaghettini
4 tbs. olive oil
2 cloves garlic
1 large can plum tomatoes
1 small eggplant, diced
1 tbs. capers (washed)
2 leaves sweet basil, chopped
½ cup grated Pecorino cheese
2 tbs. chopped green olives
Salt and pepper to taste

Heat olive oil in saucepan; brown garlic 2 minutes; then add tomatoes, salt and pepper to taste. Stir. Add olives, capers, and basil. Cover pan and simmer over very low flame 45 minutes. Add diced eggplant; simmer 20 minutes longer or until eggplant is tender.

Cook spaghettini 12 minutes in 4 quarts of rapidly boiling salted water. When tender, drain; arrange on hot platter. Pour hot sauce over this; sprinkle with grated Pecorino cheese.

Serve very hot. Serves 4 to 6.

TAGLIARINI CON FEGATINI

NARROW NOODLES WITH CHICKEN LIVERS

¾ lb. tagliarini (narrow noodles)
¾ lb. chicken livers
4 tbs. olive oil
½ cup grated Incanestrato cheese
1 large can tomatoes
1 cup cooked or canned peas
1 clove garlic, chopped
Salt and pepper to taste

Chop livers; brown in hot oil. Add garlic, salt, pepper, and tomatoes. Cover; simmer slowly for 40 minutes. Add peas; simmer for 20 minutes longer.

Cook noodles in rapidly boiling salted water, as usual. When tender, drain; arrange on heated platter and pour hot sauce over them. Sprinkle with grated Incanestrato cheese.

Serve very hot. Serves 4.

TAGLIARINI CON SPARAGI

NARROW EGG NOODLES WITH ASPARAGUS

1 lb. narrow egg noodles
2 lbs. fresh asparagus
4 tbs. olive oil
1 large can plum tomatoes
½ cup grated Parmesan cheese
2 small cloves garlic
Salt and pepper to taste

Clean asparagus and remove tough stalks. Cut in half. Dry them.

Heat olive oil in large saucepan. Add garlic and asparagus; sauté 10 minutes over low flame. Add tomatoes, salt and pepper to taste; cover; simmer slowly 1 hour. Stir occasionally to prevent burning.

Cook noodles about 12 minutes or until tender in 5 quarts of rapidly boiling salted water. Drain; place on hot platter; cover with sauce and asparagus. Sprinkle generously with grated Parmesan cheese.

Serve very hot. Serves 4 to 6.

TORTA DI DITALI

DITALI PIE

¾ lb. cooked ditali (pasta)
1½ cups Plain Tomato Sauce
½ cup grated Romano cheese
1 cup cooked chopped meat
2 eggs
Salt and pepper to taste

Make a rich flaky pastry as for pie. Line a 10-inch deep-dish pie plate or casserole.

Mix cooked ditali, tomato sauce, cheese, and meat; place over pastry. Beat eggs thoroughly; pour evenly over all. Cover with pastry; bake in moderate oven about 25 minutes or until pastry is golden brown.

Cut in individual portions and serve hot, with mixed salad. Serves 6.

CHAPTER SEVEN

Sauces

SALSA CON ACCIUGHE

ANCHOVY SAUCE

10 anchovies (filets)
2 tbs. vinegar
1 clove garlic
2 tbs. olive oil
4 hard-boiled egg yolks
½ cup chopped parsley

Put anchovies, garlic, and oil in pan; cook slowly about 5 minutes or until anchovies are dissolved. Gradually add parsley, vinegar, mashed egg yolks; stir constantly to blend well. If too thick, add a tablespoon of hot water and a tablespoon of vinegar. Stir. Remove from fire. Cool.

Serve cold on cold meats or fish.

SALSA DI CAPPERI

CAPER SAUCE

1 oz. capers
2 ozs. butter
1 tsp. flour
2 tbs. vinegar
1 tsp. chopped parsley
½ cup meat broth
Salt and pepper to taste

Wash and chop capers. Place butter in saucepan; heat over low flame. Gradually add flour, stirring constantly until smooth, light brown. Add capers, vinegar, parsley, salt and pepper to taste; stir constantly. Add broth. Simmer for 10 minutes. Serve hot over boiled or baked fish.

SALSA CON CARNE

MEAT SAUCE

1 can tomato paste
2 tbs. olive oil
1 clove garlic
2½ cups warm water
1 chopped onion
1 bay leaf
½ lb. chopped lean beef or pork
Salt and pepper to taste

Brown onion, garlic, and meat in olive oil in saucepan for about 10 minutes. Add paste; stir; cook 3 minutes longer. Add salt and pepper, water, bay leaf. Cover; simmer for 1 hour. Remove bay leaf; simmer 30 minutes longer.

SALSO CON CARNE E FUNGHI

MEAT AND MUSHROOM SAUCE

½ lb. chopped beef
¼ cup olive oil
½ can tomato paste
⅛ tsp. crushed red pepper seeds
1 cup boiled sliced mushrooms
1 clove garlic
1 large can plum tomatoes
Salt to taste

Heat oil in saucepan; add mushrooms, garlic, pepper seeds, beef; simmer 5 minutes; stir frequently. Add tomatoes; simmer over low flame for 45 minutes. Stir occasionally; add tomato paste and blend; stir; add salt. Cover. Simmer for 30 minutes more; stir occasionally to prevent sticking. The longer this cooks, the better the flavor. Keep hot over very low flame until ready to use. This is enough sauce for 1½ pounds of spaghetti or any type macaroni. Serves 6 to 8.

SALSA DI FUNGHI E POMODORO

MUSHROOM AND TOMATO SAUCE

1 lb. mushrooms
1 large can plum tomatoes
4 tbs. olive oil
2 sweet basil leaves
1 large clove garlic
Pinch of crushed red pepper seeds
Salt to taste

Wash and slice mushrooms. Place olive oil in saucepan; brown garlic 2 minutes. Add mushrooms; simmer for 10 minutes. Mash tomatoes and add; stir; add pepper seeds, basil leaves, and salt. Cover. Simmer for 1 hour over low flame. Stir occasionally to prevent sticking. Pour over spaghetti when steaming hot. Enough sauce for 1½ pounds of any type pasta. Sprinkle with Pecorino cheese if desired.

SALSA PICCANTE

PIQUANT SAUCE

1 cup burgundy or dry sauterne
1 cup olive oil
2 chopped onions
Pinch of rosemary
2 cloves garlic, chopped
¼ cup wine vinegar
⅛ tsp. dried red pepper seeds
¼ tsp. salt

Mix all ingredients thoroughly. Stir constantly until well blended. Put in jar to marinate for 24 hours. Remove garlic. Good with cold meats and fowl. Also may be used to baste meats and fowl while roasting or broiling. Imparts exotic flavor.

SALSA DI PISELLI

PEA SAUCE

3 tbs. olive oil
1 sliced onion
1 strip bacon, chopped
1 tsp. chopped parsley
2 cups fresh peas, shelled
1 cup water
Salt and pepper to taste

Cook onion in olive oil about 5 minutes or until soft. Add chopped bacon; simmer 3 minutes. Add parsley; stir. Add water and peas, salt and pepper; cook slowly for 20 minutes or until peas are done.

This sauce may be used on any type macaroni or rice. Grated Parmesan cheese may also be sprinkled over top for added flavor.

SALSA SEMPLICE DI POMODORO #1

PLAIN TOMATO SAUCE #1

1 large can tomatoes
4 tbs. olive oil
2 sliced onions
½ tsp. sugar
1 clove garlic
1 sprig sweet basil
Salt and pepper to taste

Fry sliced onion and garlic in oil about 5 minutes; add basil. Strain tomatoes through sieve; add and simmer for 45 minutes or until tomatoes are cooked to a thick sauce. Stir frequently. Add sugar, salt, and pepper; stir thoroughly. Simmer 15 minutes.

This sauce may be used on any type macaroni or boiled rice. Sufficient for 1 pound. Also used with Pizza recipe.

SALSA SEMPLICE DI POMODORO #2

PLAIN TOMATO SAUCE #2

1 can tomato paste
3 tbs. olive oil
2 large onions, sliced
½ tsp. orégano
2½ cups water
Salt and pepper to taste

Fry onion in oil about 5 minutes or until medium brown. Add paste; fry 3 minutes, stirring constantly. Add orégano, salt and pepper to taste; also 2½ cups water; cover. Simmer over low flame for 25 minutes.

Easily and quickly prepared. May be used on any type macaroni. Sufficient for 1 pound. Serve very hot.

SALSA TARTUFATA

TRUFFLE SAUCE

½ cup sliced truffles
¾ cup bouillon or broth
¼ cup dry sherry
2 tbs. butter
1 tsp. flour
1 tsp. chopped parsley
1 sliced onion
1 small clove garlic
Salt and pepper to taste

Place butter in saucepan and melt over low flame. Brown garlic, onion, and parsley lightly for about 2 minutes. Blend flour with sherry and add; lower flame; stir constantly until very smooth. Add truffles, bouillon, salt and pepper to taste; cover; simmer for about 20 minutes. Excellent over roasts and veal cutlets. Serve hot.

SALSA DI VONGOLI

CLAM SAUCE

1 doz. little-neck clams
2 cloves garlic
1 tbs. chopped parsley
4 tbs. olive oil
1 large can tomatoes
Salt and pepper to taste

Scrub clams; rinse in cold running water until all sand is removed. Insert thin knife blade between edges of shells and pry open. Cut clams into small pieces. Place clams with juice in bowl.

Brown garlic in hot oil in saucepan; add clam juice, strained tomatoes, chopped parsley, salt and pepper to taste. Simmer slowly for 40 minutes; add clams; turn up flame; cook for only 2 minutes. Prolonged cooking toughens clams.

Enough for 4 to 6 portions. Sufficient sauce for 1 pound of spaghetti or other macaroni. Grated cheese is not generally used with this sauce.

CHAPTER EIGHT

Sea Foods

Fish

BACCALÀ DOLCE E AGRO

DRY COD SWEET AND SOUR

1 whole dry cod (about 2 lbs.)
2 tbs. currants or seedless raisins
1 tbs. shelled pistachio nuts
½ cup olive or peanut oil
1 clove garlic
½ cup flour
½ cup vinegar
⅔ cup water
1 tbs. chopped fresh mint
Pinch of pepper

Soak cod in cold water 24 hours. Change water several times. Wash in cold water before using. Dry with absorbent paper; cut in serving pieces. Roll in flour.

Heat oil in skillet; brown garlic 3 minutes; remove from oil. Fry cod in hot oil about 5 minutes on each side or until light brown and tender.

In separate saucepan blend vinegar, water, currants, mint, and pistachio nuts; boil slowly 5 minutes. Pour hot sauce over cod; cover; simmer slowly 3 minutes.

Serve very hot with green salad. Serves 4.

BACCALÀ FIORENTINA

DRY COD FLORENTINE

1 whole dry cod (about 2 lbs.)
2 cloves garlic
3 tbs. tomato paste
2 sprigs fresh mint
1 tsp. washed capers
½ cup olive or peanut oil
½ cup flour
1 cup warm water
Pinch of pepper to taste

Soak fish in cold water 24 hours. Change water several times. Wash in cold water before cooking.

Cut fish in 4-inch serving pieces. Roll in flour.

Heat oil in skillet; brown garlic 3 minutes; fry cod 3 or 4 minutes on each side until light brown. Sprinkle lightly with pepper to taste.

Blend tomato paste with warm water; pour over fish; add mint and capers; cover; simmer about 10 minutes or until tender and well done.

Serve very hot. Serves 4.

CALAMAI CON POMODORO

SQUIDS WITH TOMATOES

2 lbs. squids
4 tbs. olive oil
Pinch of orégano
1 tsp. chopped parsley
1 cup solid-pack tomatoes
½ cup dry sherry
2 cloves garlic
Salt and pepper to taste

Have squids thoroughly cleaned. Cut into small pieces. Wash well.

Pour olive oil in saucepan and heat; brown garlic about 3 minutes. Add squids; cover; sauté 10 minutes. Add salt, pepper, orégano, and sherry; cook 10 minutes longer over low flame. Add tomatoes, parsley; cover; cook 15 minutes or until tender.

Serve very hot on toast. Serves 4 to 6.

CAPITONE FRITTO

FRIED EELS

2½ lbs. thick eels
6 tbs. olive oil
1 cup flour
1 tsp. rosemary
Salt and pepper to taste

Have eels skinned and cleaned. Cut crosswise in 3-inch pieces. Dry; roll in flour; add salt and pepper. Sprinkle with rosemary. Fry over medium flame about 10 minutes or until golden brown on both sides.

Serve hot with lemon slices. Serves 4 to 6.

This is a Christmas Eve specialty.

ANGUILLE MARINATE

MARINATED EELS

Follow same procedure as for fried eels (Capitone Fritto). Put fried eels in deep dish. Then prepare this dressing:

¾ cup wine vinegar
¾ cup water
1 clove garlic
1 large onion, sliced
1 bay leaf
Pinch of rosemary
Salt and pepper to taste

Strain and use leftover oil after frying eels.

Combine vinegar and water; boil for 2 minutes; sauté garlic and onion in hot oil about 5 minutes or until medium soft. Add vinegar, water, bay leaf, rosemary, salt and pepper to taste; cook 5 minutes over low flame. Remove; cool. Pour prepared liquid over eels. Set aside in refrigerator.

May be served cold at any time. Marinating the eels several hours improves the flavor.

MERLUZZO LESSO

BOILED WHITING

2 lbs. whiting
1 clove garlic, chopped
2 tbs. chopped parsley
3 tbs. olive oil
1½ cups warm water
Salt and pepper to taste

Have fish cleaned. Wash thoroughly. Cut in half crosswise. Place olive oil, parsley, and garlic in saucepan; cook about 3 minutes or until garlic is soft. Add warm water and allow to come to a boil. Add fish, salt, and pepper;

cover; simmer 10 minutes over low flame. Serve in own broth.

Serve very hot. Serves 4.

MERLUZZO CON SALSA DI POMODORO

WHITING WITH TOMATO SAUCE

2 lbs. whiting
1 clove garlic, chopped
2 tbs. chopped parsley
1 No. 2 can tomatoes
1 minced onion
1 diced carrot
4 tbs. olive oil
Salt and pepper to taste

Have fish cleaned. Wash thoroughly. Cut crosswise, in half. Brown onion and garlic in oil; add carrot and parsley; cook slowly 5 minutes. Add tomatoes, salt, and pepper; cover; cook over slow flame 25 minutes longer. Add fish; cover; continue cooking slowly 10 minutes or until fish is tender.

Serve very hot with sauce. Serves 4.

FRITELLE DI PESCIOLINI

MINNOW PANCAKES

1 lb. minnows
2 eggs
1 clove garlic, chopped
1 tbs. chopped parsley
½ cup peanut oil
3 tbs. grated Romano cheese
1 cup flour
¼ cup bread crumbs
1 tsp. chopped sweet basil
Salt and pepper to taste

Wash and clean minnows. Drain. Place in deep mixing bowl. Add eggs, salt, pepper, cheese, basil, parsley, bread crumbs, and garlic. Add enough flour for easy molding. Form into small pancakes, about 3 inches in diameter. Roll in flour.

Pour oil in skillet and heat; fry pancakes quickly, about 5 minutes or until golden brown.

Serve very hot. Serves 4.

SALMONE LESSO

BOILED SALMON

2 lbs. salmon
3 cups water
1 tbs. chopped parsley
1 sliced carrot
3 tbs. olive oil
1 sliced onion
2 cloves
1 sliced lemon
½ cup diced celery
Salt and pepper to taste

Have salmon sliced about 2 inches thick.

Boil all ingredients except salmon and lemon about 20 minutes. Add salmon; cover; cook 15 minutes or until tender.

Serve very hot with own broth. Garnish with lemon slices. Serves 4.

SARDE BECCAFICO

STUFFED SARDINES

2 lbs. fresh sardines

Clean each sardine carefully. Slit down center to form an open filet and remove bones.

Stuffing:

1½ cups bread crumbs
2 tbs. chopped parsley
4 tbs. olive oil
¼ cup grated Romano cheese
1 clove garlic, chopped
Salt and pepper to taste

Mix thoroughly all ingredients except olive oil; gradually add oil to make a firm mixture. If needed, add another teaspoon of oil.

Cover whole filet with stuffing; top with another filet to form a sandwich. Tie with white thread so stuffing does not fall out. Continue this until all are used.

Sauce:

3 tbs. olive oil
1 tbs. chopped sweet basil or parsley
1 clove garlic, chopped
1 No. 2 can tomato purée
Salt and pepper to taste

Pour olive oil in large shallow pan; add garlic, parsley or basil; cook 3 minutes. Add tomato purée, salt and pepper to taste; simmer over slow fire 25 minutes. Stir frequently. Place fish very carefully in sauce; cover pan; cook over low flame 15 minutes or until fish is tender.

Prepare hot platter. Remove fish carefully and put on platter. Remove thread by cutting; pour sauce over fish.

Serve very hot. Serves 4 to 6.

SGOMBRO RIPIENO

STUFFED MACKEREL

3 mackerel (about 1 lb. each)
6 tbs. olive oil
1 chopped onion
1 cup bread crumbs
¼ cup grated Romano cheese
¼ cup fresh mushrooms, chopped
1 tbs. chopped parsley
1 tsp. fresh mint, chopped
1 sliced lemon
Salt and pepper to taste

Have fish cleaned, slit down center, and boned. Sprinkle inside with salt.

Stuffing: Heat half of olive oil in saucepan. Sauté onion, mushrooms, and parsley about 15 minutes or until mushrooms are tender. Set aside.

Mix in deep bowl the bread crumbs, mint, cheese, salt and pepper to taste. Add to mushroom mixture. Blend well. Stuff fish. Skewer or sew edges together; place stuffed fish with balance of oil in baking pan; bake in hot oven 15 minutes; reduce heat. Baste occasionally with pan oil and cook 15 minutes longer or until fish is tender.

Serve very hot with lemon slices. Serves 4 to 6.

SPADA ALLA GRIGLIA

BROILED SWORDFISH

2 lbs. swordfish
Juice of 2 lemons
1 tsp. fresh mint, chopped
¼ cup olive oil
2 tsp. orégano
Salt and pepper to taste

Have fish sliced 1½ inches thick. Wash. Dry.

Blend well oil, lemon juice, orégano, mint, salt, and pepper. Brush fish with this.

Place on preheated broiler rack about 4 inches below flame.

Broil 5 minutes or until slightly brown; turn; brush again with mixture. Broil about 7 minutes or until done. Brush again with mixture before serving.

Serve hot. Serves 4 to 6.

FILETTI DI SOGLIOLE PIZZAIOLA

FILET OF SOLE PIZZAIOLA*

1 lb. filet of sole
1 tbs. orégano
1 tbs. chopped parsley
Juice of 1 lemon
½ cup bread crumbs
½ cup canned plum tomatoes
Salt and pepper to taste
¼ cup olive oil or melted butter

Blend thoroughly bread crumbs, orégano, parsley, salt and pepper to taste. Roll fish in this mixture.

Put half of oil or butter in baking dish; place breaded filet in dish. Spread tomatoes over fish; pour balance of oil or melted butter over this.

Bake in hot oven 10 minutes or until tender. Serve steaming hot with lemon juice. Serves 4.

* Aunt Lena's recipe. *Pizzaiola* means "like a little pie."

SPINOLA RIPIENA

STUFFED STRIPED BASS

1 striped bass (about 4 lbs.)
5 tbs. olive oil
2 cups bread crumbs
1 large onion, chopped
Juice of 1 lemon
1 tsp. thyme
Pinch of marjoram
3 tbs. grated Romano cheese
½ cup chopped celery
1 small clove garlic, chopped
Salt and pepper to taste

Have fish cleaned, slit down center, and boned. Sprinkle inside with salt.

Stuffing: Place 3 tablespoons olive oil in saucepan; add celery, onion, and garlic; cook about 10 minutes or until soft. Remove from fire.

Mix thoroughly in bowl bread crumbs, salt, pepper, thyme, cheese, marjoram; add this to celery, onion, and garlic. Blend well. Stuff fish. Skewer or sew edges together to prevent stuffing from falling out. Place in baking pan. Brush fish with remaining oil. Bake in hot oven 10 minutes. Then lower heat; bake in moderate oven about 20 minutes or until fish is tender. If pan gets too dry, add about ¼ cup hot water. Baste fish. Add lemon juice before serving.

Serve very hot. Serves 6.

STOCCO SCIACCA

STOCKFISH SCIACCA

2 lbs. soaked stockfish
1 tsp. orégano
1 tbs. capers
1 tbs. chopped sweet basil
½ cup olive oil
1 No. 2 can tomatoes
10 ripe black olives
1 clove garlic
Salt and pepper to taste

Cut stockfish† into serving pieces about 3 inches long. Wash in cold running water; dry with absorbent paper.

† Stockfish, a species of dry cod, may be purchased in Italian fish markets. It is soaked and prepared for use as given in this recipe.

Fry in ¼ cup of oil 10 minutes or until golden brown on both sides. Remove from pan.

Meanwhile, cook garlic 2 minutes in balance of oil in saucepan; when light brown add tomatoes, salt, and pepper; cover; cook for 20 minutes over low flame. Add fish, olives, basil, capers, orégano; cook 15 minutes.

Serve very hot. Serves 6.

STOCCO PALERMITANA

STOCKFISH PALERMO

2 lbs. soaked stockfish
1 cup stewed or canned tomatoes
1 tbs. washed capers
1 sliced onion
½ lb. diced potatoes
½ cup olive oil
¼ lb. chopped green olives
½ cup diced celery
Salt and pepper to taste

Cut soaked stockfish into 3-inch pieces. Wash in cold running water.

Heat oil in large saucepan; sauté fish and all ingredients except tomatoes for 15 minutes. Stir frequently. Add tomatoes and enough warm water to cover all. Lower flame; add very little salt, pepper; cover; cook slowly about 10 minutes or until fish and potatoes are tender.

Serve hot. Serves 6.

TONNO AGRO E DOLCE

TUNA SOUR AND SWEET

2 lbs. fresh tuna fish
½ cup peanut or olive oil
2 large onions, sliced
6 tbs. wine vinegar
1½ tsp. sugar
Salt and pepper to taste
4 sprigs fresh mint or sweet basil, chopped

Have tuna fish sliced 1½ inches thick. Season with salt and pepper to taste. Pour oil in skillet; heat; fry fish about 10 minutes or until brown on both sides. Remove fish. Set aside.

Cook onion slowly in same oil about 5 minutes or until soft; add vinegar, mint or basil, and sugar. Cover; cook slowly 5 minutes more. Place fish in hot sauce; cover; cook slowly 3 minutes longer. Serve very hot.

Fish may also be served cold. If so, cool sauce; pour over fish; marinate several hours in cool place. The longer it marinates, the better the flavor.

Serves 4 to 6.

TONNO ALLA GRIGLIA

BROILED TUNA FISH

2 lbs. fresh tuna fish
4 tbs. olive oil
½ clove garlic chopped
1½ cups bread crumbs
1 tbs. chopped parsley
1 tsp. fresh mint, chopped
1 lemon
Salt and pepper to taste

Have fish sliced 1½ inches thick. Wash; dry with damp cloth. Rub with a little oil; sprinkle lightly with salt and pepper.

Mix bread crumbs, garlic, parsley, and mint. Roll fish in this mixture. Pour a little oil over each slice. Place on preheated broiler rack, about 4 inches below medium flame; broil about 7 minutes on each side or until tender.

Serve very hot with lemon slices. Serves 4.

TONNO CON SALSA DI POMODORO

FRESH TUNA WITH TOMATO SAUCE

2 lbs. fresh tuna fish
4 tbs. olive oil
1 tbs. chopped parsley
2 cups hot water
1 clove garlic
1 small onion, sliced
½ can tomato paste
Salt and pepper to taste

Have fish sliced 1½ inches thick. Wash; dry with absorbent paper; sprinkle with salt and pepper to taste.

Pour oil in skillet; add onion, garlic, parsley; cook 5 minutes or until soft.

Blend tomato paste in 2 cups of hot water; add to mixture in skillet; cover; simmer 20 minutes, stirring occasionally. Add fish; cover; cook 15 minutes or until tender.

Serve very hot. Serves 4.

TROTA CON ACCIUGHE

TROUT WITH ANCHOVY

6 trout
6 tbs. olive oil
4 filets of anchovy
1 cup dry sherry
Juice of 1 lemon
1 cup flour
3 tbs. butter
1 tsp. fresh mint, chopped
1 tsp. chopped parsley
Salt and pepper to taste

Clean trout; dry with absorbent paper; salt and pepper to taste; roll in flour. Fry slowly in hot olive oil about 10 minutes or until brown.

Melt butter in saucepan over low flame. Add anchovy filets cut into small pieces; cook about 5 minutes. Add sherry; cover; simmer 1 minute. Add mint and parsley; simmer 3 minutes. Add lemon juice.

Place fish on hot platter; pour sauce over it. Serve very hot. Serves 4 to 6.

Shellfish

ARAGOSTA FRA DIAVOLO

LOBSTER FRA DIAVOLO

2 lobsters (about 1½ lbs. each)
2 tbs. chopped parsley
1 clove garlic, chopped
2 cups canned plum tomatoes
¼ cup olive oil
¼ tsp. crushed red pepper seeds
1 tsp. orégano
Salt and pepper to taste

Insert sharp knife between body and tail of lobster to sever spinal cord. Place on back and split to end of tail. Spread open. The green and coral parts are edible, but be sure to remove the small sac just back of the head. Crack large claws.

Place lobster cut side up in large flat baking dish. Set aside.

Pour olive oil in saucepan; heat; brown garlic 2 minutes. Add tomatoes, parsley, orégano, pepper seeds, salt, and very little pepper. Simmer 10 minutes. Pour sauce evenly over top of lobster. Bake in moderately hot oven about 20 minutes or until lobster meat is tender.

Serve very hot. Serves 4.

ARAGOSTA ALLA MARSALA

LOBSTER MARSALA

1 large lobster (1½ lbs.)
1 tbs. chopped parsley
½ cup marsala
4 tbs. olive oil
2 cloves garlic
Salt and pepper to taste

Insert sharp knife between body and tail of lobster to sever spinal cord. Do not remove from shell. Clean; cut into small serving pieces; crack claws.

Pour oil in saucepan; brown garlic about 3 minutes; remove from oil. Add lobster, salt and pepper, parsley. Cover; simmer over low flame for 20 minutes or until tender. Add marsala; simmer 2 minutes.

Serve very hot. Serves 2.

ARAGOSTA OREGANATA

LOBSTER ORÉGANO

1 large lobster (about 2 lbs.)
6 tbs. olive oil
1 clove garlic, chopped
1 tsp. chopped sweet basil
1 tbs. chopped parsley
2 tbs. grated Parmesan cheese
½ tsp. orégano
½ cup bread crumbs
Salt and pepper to taste

Insert sharp knife between body and tail of lobster to sever spinal cord. Place on back and split to end of tail. Spread open. The green and coral parts are edible, but be sure to remove the small sac just back of the head. Crack large claws.

Place in baking pan, cut side up; add ½ cup water to pan.

Mix thoroughly bread crumbs, parsley, basil, cheese, orégano, and garlic. Sprinkle evenly over lobster; add salt and pepper to taste. Pour oil over all.

Place on broiler rack about 6 inches below medium flame. Broil about 20 minutes or until lobster meat is tender.

Serve very hot. Serves 2.

ARAGOSTA MARINARA

LOBSTER MARINER

1 large lobster (2 lbs.)
5 tbs. olive oil
2 whole cloves garlic
½ cup dry sherry
1 tbs. chopped parsley
1 No. 2 can tomatoes
1 sliced onion
Salt and pepper to taste

Insert sharp knife between body and tail of lobster to sever spinal cord. Place on back; split. Spread open; cut crosswise for convenience in cooking. The green and coral parts are edible, but be sure to remove the small sac just back of the head. Crack large claws.

Brown garlic and onion in saucepan with olive oil; remove garlic. Add lobster; cover; cook over low flame 10 minutes or until shell is red. Remove lobster; set aside.

Put tomatoes in same pan. Add parsley, salt, and pepper; cover; simmer slowly for 15 minutes.

While sauce is cooking remove lobster from shell and cut into small pieces. When sauce is done add lobster; cover; simmer slowly 10 minutes more. Add sherry.

Serve very hot. Serves 2.

GAMBERI ALLA MARIO

SHRIMP MARIO

2 lbs. large fresh shrimp
1 cup flour
1 large green pepper
¾ cup dry sherry
½ cup olive oil
Salt and pepper to taste

Clean and stem pepper; cut into ½-inch pieces.

Clean shrimp and remove shells. Dip in flour and fry in very hot oil about 5 minutes or until brown on both sides. Add salt and pepper to taste. Remove from pan.

Fry pepper in same oil about 10 minutes. When soft, add shrimp; simmer for 2 minutes. Stir. Add sherry; cover; cook 3 minutes over high flame.

Serve with broccoli and buttered rice. Serves 4.

GAMBERI CON RISO

SHRIMP WITH RICE

3 cups boiled rice
4 tbs. olive oil
2 sliced onions
1 tsp. chopped sweet basil
2 cups boiled shrimp
1 No. 2 can solid-pack tomatoes
2 cups fresh cooked peas
½ cup diced celery
Salt and pepper to taste

Pour oil in deep saucepan and heat. Add onion and celery; cook about 10 minutes over medium flame, or until soft. Add tomatoes, basil, salt, and pepper. Cook slowly 20 minutes. Stir occasionally. Add peas, shrimp. Cover; cook 5 minutes longer or until shrimp is thoroughly heated.

Place about ½ cup hot rice on individual heated plates; top with shrimp mixture.

Serve very hot. Serves 4 to 6.

LUMACHE SICILIANA

SNAILS SICILIAN

2 lbs. snails
1 clove garlic
1 large chopped onion
1 tbs. chopped parsley
4 tbs. olive oil
½ can tomato paste
2 cups hot water
Salt and pepper to taste

Place snails in large deep pot. Cover with cold water. Rub rim of salt around the inside of pot just below the edge to prevent snails from coming out of water.

Soak for ½ hour. Then wash thoroughly in several waters. Drain well. Use only live snails with heads out of shell.

Pour oil in deep pot. Heat; add onion and garlic; cook slowly 3 minutes or until soft. Remove garlic. Add tomato paste; cook over low flame for 5 minutes, stirring constantly. Add hot water and blend. Add snails; stir; sauté over moderate flame 10 minutes. Add salt and pepper to taste; stir. Add parsley; cover; simmer slowly 20 minutes.

Serve very hot in deep plates with the sauce. (Use small oyster fork or nut pick to extract snail.) Serves 6 to 8.

OSTRICHE ALLA MARIO

OYSTERS MARIO

2 doz. large oysters
3 tbs. butter
2 tbs. olive oil
2 tbs. chopped parsley
1 clove garlic
1 cup bread crumbs
½ tsp. orégano
Juice of 1 lemon
Salt and pepper to taste

Scrub shells; rinse in cold running water. Insert knife blade between edges of shells, cutting through the muscle of oyster. Pry open. Remove from shells.

Rub the half shell with garlic and tiny piece of butter; replace oyster. Sprinkle with salt and pepper.

Mix bread crumbs, olive oil, parsley, and orégano. Sprinkle this mixture on each oyster. Arrange in pan; bake in moderate oven 10 minutes or until edges of oysters curl.

Serve very hot with lemon juice. Serves 4.

VONGOLI SU PANE ABBRUSTOLITO

CLAMS ON TOAST

2 doz. clams
2 cloves garlic, chopped
1 tsp. chopped parsley
4 slices toast
¼ tsp. orégano
½ cup water
2 cups canned tomatoes
4 tbs. olive oil
Salt and pepper to taste

Scrub clams with stiff brush; rinse in cold running water until all sand is removed. Place in large pot; add water; cover; cook slowly 20 minutes or until shells open. Remove clams from shells.

Place oil in saucepan; heat; brown garlic about 2 minutes. Add tomatoes, parsley, orégano, salt, and pepper. Cook slowly for 20 minutes; stir to prevent sticking. Add steamed clams; cook 1 minute longer.

Place on toast and serve very hot. Serves 4.

VONGOLI SICILIANA

STEAMED CLAMS SICILIAN

2 doz. clams in shells
2 tbs. parsley
2 cloves garlic
2 tbs. olive oil
½ cup water
Salt and pepper to taste

Scrub clams with stiff brush; rinse in running water until all sand is removed.

Place garlic, oil, and parsley in large pot; heat 3 minutes. Add water, a little salt and pepper to taste, and clams. Cover; steam over medium flame about 20 minutes or until shells open. Place clams in deep plates.

Serve hot with clam broth. Serves 4.

(Steamed clams may be used on spaghetti with Plain Tomato Sauce. Steam as shown here. Remove from shells; cut clams into small pieces; add to sauce.)

CHAPTER NINE

Meats

Beef

BISTECCA MILANESE

BEEFSTEAK MILANESE

1 sirloin steak (about 3 lbs.)
1 clove garlic
3 tbs. butter
2 tbs. olive oil
Salt and pepper to taste

Sprinkle steak with pepper. Heat skillet. Melt butter; add oil. Brown garlic about 1 minute; remove garlic from pan. Brown steak on each side about 5 minutes over high flame if rare steak is desired, or 7 to 10 minutes for medium rare. Remove from fire. Sprinkle with salt to taste; pour pan gravy over steak while sizzling hot.

Serve immediately. Serves 4 to 6.

BRACIUOLINI DI MANZO

BROILED BEEF ROLLETTES

1½ lbs. top round steak
3 strips bacon
1 large onion, sliced
2 cloves garlic
2 tsp. chopped parsley
Salt and pepper to taste

Have steak sliced very thin (about ¼ inch) and cut into 3-inch squares. Place small piece of garlic, slice of onion, pinch of parsley, and 1-inch piece of bacon in center of each square. Roll carefully so ingredients do not ooze out. Top with small piece of bacon. Fasten each roll together with toothpicks.

Place on broiler rack about 5 inches below flame and broil about 5 minutes on each side or until golden brown and tender. Sprinkle with salt and pepper.

Serve very hot. Serves 4 to 6.

POLPETTE

MEAT BALLS

1 lb. chopped beef
3 tbs. grated Romano cheese
2 tbs. chopped parsley
6 tbs. olive oil
3 eggs
3 slices stale bread
1 clove garlic, chopped
Salt and pepper to taste

Soak bread in water 5 minutes; squeeze dry. Mix thoroughly with meat, slightly beaten eggs, grated Romano cheese, garlic, and parsley. Add salt and pepper to taste. Shape into balls about size of small egg; roll in flour; fry in hot oil about 10 minutes or until golden brown.

Serve very hot with vegetables and salad. May also be served with Spaghetti and Plain Tomato Sauce. Serves 4 to 6.

FILETTO SICILIANA

FILET MIGNON SICILIAN

2 lbs. filet mignon
1 medium onion, sliced
2 slices bacon
1/8 lb. butter
1/2 cup marsala (sherry)
Salt and pepper to taste

Have filet sliced 1½ inches thick.

Heat skillet; brown bacon slightly. Add onion; brown 2 minutes. Remove bacon and onion. Brown filet over high flame about 5 minutes on each side. Lower flame; continue frying 5 minutes; add salt and pepper to taste.

Melt butter in separate pan; pour over filet. Add marsala; simmer 2 minutes.

Serve very hot. Serves 4.

MANZO ALLA MODA

BEEF À LA MODE

4 lbs. top sirloin or eye round (in 1 piece)
2 large carrots, diced
1 tbs. chopped parsley
2 large onions, sliced
2 tbs. olive oil
1 clove
2 ozs. butter
1 cup burgundy
3 tbs. tomato paste
2 cups hot water
Salt and pepper to taste

Heat olive oil and butter in deep pot. When very hot, brown meat quickly on all sides, about 15 minutes. Add onions, carrots, parsley, and clove; cook for 5 minutes; stir. Dissolve tomato paste in cup of hot water; add. Season to taste. Cover. Cook over low flame for 1¼ hours. Turn meat frequently to prevent scorching.

Add burgundy; cook for 15 minutes longer. Gradually add balance of water; cover; simmer for ¼ hour or until meat is very tender.

Slice; serve very hot. Serves 6 to 8.

SPIEDINI ALLA ROMANA

SKEWERED CHOPPED BEEF ROMAN STYLE

Meat Mixture Ingredients:

1 lb. chopped beef (top round)
2 eggs
3 tbs. grated Romano cheese
½ cup bread crumbs
2 tbs. chopped parsley
1 clove garlic, chopped
Salt and pepper to taste

Mix all meat ingredients thoroughly. Mold into oblong shapes 2 inches long and 1 inch in diameter. Set aside on platter.

Other Ingredients:

1 lb. Mozzarella cheese
¼ lb. prosciutto (Italian ham)
2 eggs
½ cup flour
4 slices white bread
1 cup bread crumbs
½ cup peanut or olive oil
Salt and pepper to taste

Have 12 skewers ready. Cut bread, prosciutto, and Mozzarella into 1-inch squares and place on separate plates. Thread each skewer alternately with oblong meat shapes, bread, prosciutto, and Mozzarella. Set aside. Break eggs into deep oblong dish; beat thoroughly. Place bread crumbs and flour on convenient flat board. Dip filled skewer in flour, then in egg, and finally in bread crumbs. Set all aside on platter. Place oil in very large frying pan; when well heated, fry *spiedini* (filled skewers) quickly about 5 minutes on each side or until golden brown but not dry.

Serve on skewers while still sizzling hot. Serves 6.

Lamb

AGNELLINO AL FORNO

ROASTED WHOLE BABY LAMB

1 baby lamb (about 8 lbs.)
12 strips bacon
3 large tart apples
6 cloves garlic
2 whole cloves
1 large onion, sliced
Salt and pepper to taste

Have lamb cleaned, dressed, and slit for stuffing. Rub lightly, inside and out, with salt and pepper. With point of sharp knife make 3 small openings on each side of lamb; insert small pieces of bacon and garlic. Stuff lamb with three whole peeled apples, 4 strips of bacon, and 2 whole cloves. Sew or skewer to prevent stuffing from falling out. Place lamb in roasting pan; put balance of bacon strips and onion over it; brown in hot oven about 30 minutes. Baste frequently until whole lamb is golden brown. Then lower heat; roast about 1½ hours or until tender. Baste occasionally. If pan becomes dry, add little water.

Serve very hot. Serves 6 to 8.

If preferred, lamb may be broiled over charcoal on a spit.

At Easter time whole baby lambs may be purchased from Italian butchers.

BRACIUOLINI D'AGNELLO

LAMB ROLLETTES

1¼ lbs. lamb steak
2 cloves garlic
1 large onion, sliced
4 tbs. olive oil
Pinch of rosemary
½ cup dry sauterne
Salt and pepper to taste

Have lamb sliced very thin (about ¼ inch) and cut into 3-inch squares.

Sprinkle lamb lightly with salt and pepper; place small piece of garlic and slice of onion in center of each square; roll and fasten with toothpicks.

Heat olive oil in skillet; brown rolls quickly about 5 minutes or until golden color. Sprinkle pinch of rosemary over all; cover; cook slowly about 15 minutes or until tender. Add sauterne; simmer 3 minutes.

Serve very hot. Serves 4.

AGNELLO CON RISO

LAMB WITH RICE

2 lbs. lamb (from leg)
1 cup rice
1 large onion, sliced
¼ cup olive oil
½ can tomato paste
1 cup warm water
Salt and pepper to taste

Have lamb cut into small cubes as for stew.

Pour oil in skillet; heat. Brown lamb slightly for about

8 minutes. Add onion; cover; simmer 5 minutes or until onion is soft. Add salt and pepper.

Blend tomato paste in cup of warm water; add to lamb. Cover; simmer about 45 minutes or until tender.

In the meantime, cook rice about 20 minutes in 2 quarts of boiling water to which ½ teaspoon of salt has been added. Drain in colander; rinse with cup of cold water. Keep hot by placing colander over pot of boiling water.

Arrange rice on hot platter, leaving space in center. Place lamb in hollow; pour sauce over lamb.

Serve very hot. Serves 4 to 6.

AGNELLO IN UMIDO CON CUCUZZA

LAMB STEW WITH SQUASH

2 lbs. lean stewing lamb
4 tbs. olive oil
1½ lbs. cucuzza (light green Italian squash)
1 tsp. orégano
2 large ripe tomatoes
1 large onion, sliced
Salt and pepper to taste

Wash and scrape squash; cut into 1-inch cubes.

Dip tomatoes in boiling water 1 minute; peel.

Have lamb cut into serving pieces.

Pour oil in large saucepan; heat. Add onion; cook about 3 minutes or until soft. Add lamb; cook about 15 minutes or until brown on all sides. Add tomatoes (cut into small pieces). Add orégano, salt and pepper to taste; cover; simmer 20 minutes. Add squash; simmer 10 minutes longer or until squash is tender.

Serve very hot. Serves 4 to 6.

Pork

COSTATELLE DI MAIALE

PORK CHOPS

4 thick loin pork chops
1 cup vinegar
1 cup bread crumbs
4 tbs. olive oil
1 tbs. chopped parsley
1 clove garlic, chopped
1 large egg
½ cup flour
Salt and pepper to taste

Marinate chops in vinegar for about 1 hour in shallow dish. Remove from vinegar. Dry with absorbent paper. Sprinkle with salt and pepper.

Beat egg lightly; blend with 1 tablespoon of cold water. Mix bread crumbs, garlic and parsley, a little salt and pepper.

Roll chops in flour; dip in egg, then in bread crumbs; fry in hot oil for about 5 minutes or until brown on both sides. Lower flame; cover; continue frying slowly for 20 minutes or until well done and tender.

Serve very hot. Serves 4.

COSTATELLE DI MAIALE CON CAVOLO

PORK CHOPS AND CABBAGE

2 lbs. pork chops
2 chopped onions
1 clove garlic, chopped
1 No. 2 can tomatoes
1 lb. shredded cabbage
4 tbs. olive oil
1 cup burgundy
Salt and pepper to taste

Fry onions in hot olive oil for about 3 minutes or until soft. Remove onions; add garlic and pork chops. Turn up flame. Brown chops quickly on both sides about 6 minutes. Transfer chops, garlic, and onions to a deep pot. Add cabbage, tomatoes, salt and pepper to taste; cover tightly; cook slowly for 30 minutes. Add burgundy; continue cooking about 10 minutes, very slowly, or until cabbage and chops are tender.

Serve very hot. Serves 6.

MAIALINO ARROSTITO

ROASTED SUCKLING PIG

1 small suckling pig (about 10 lbs.)
6 cloves garlic
3 large green apples
3 large oranges
1 tsp. crushed red pepper seeds
Salt and pepper to taste

Have suckling cleaned and slit down center for stuffing. Rub lightly (inside and out) with salt and pepper. Peel and quarter oranges and green apples; place inside. Sew or skewer together.

With point of sharp knife make 3 small openings on each side; insert clove of garlic in each.

Sprinkle very lightly with crushed red pepper seeds; roast in very hot oven, watching constantly. When brown, lower heat and roast about 4 hours or until well done. Baste with pan juice from time to time to prevent dryness. When ready to serve, remove garlic; slice thickly.

Serve very hot. Serves 10 to 12.

If preferred, suckling may be roasted on spit over charcoal fire.

Orange and Lemon Salad may be served with suckling.

Veal

COSTATELLE DI VITELLA CACCIATORA

VEAL CHOPS HUNTER'S STYLE

1½ lbs. veal chops
1 tbs. butter
5 tbs. olive oil
1 stalk chopped celery
1 medium carrot, chopped
1 medium onion, chopped
1 tsp. chopped parsley
¾ cup dry sherry
1 tbs. tomato paste
Salt and pepper to taste

Melt butter and oil in hot skillet. Brown chops well on both sides (about 10 minutes). Add all chopped vegetables, salt and pepper to taste; cover; simmer about 10 minutes or until all vegetables are soft. Gradually add sherry into which tomato paste has been well blended. Stir occasionally to prevent burning or sticking. Cover. Simmer over low flame about 20 minutes or until chops are tender. While simmering, if there is insufficient gravy, add 2 tablespoons of warm water.

Serve very hot. Serves 4.

COTOLETTE ALLA PARMIGIANA

VEAL CUTLETS PARMESAN

1 lb. veal cutlets
3 tbs. grated Parmesan cheese
6 tbs. olive oil
½ lb. Mozzarella cheese
1 cup bread crumbs
2 eggs
Salt and pepper to taste

Beat eggs thoroughly; add salt and pepper. Mix bread crumbs with cheese. Dip cutlets in egg, then in bread crumbs; fry in hot oil about 5 minutes on each side or until golden brown.

Prepare Plain Tomato Sauce #1.

Place browned cutlets in baking pan; pour layer of sauce over them; then place thin slices of Mozzarella over top. Bake in slow oven for 15 minutes or until cheese turns slightly brown.

Serve very hot. Serves 4.

COTOLETTE DI VITELLA

VEAL CUTLETS

1 lb. veal cutlets
2 eggs
3 tbs. grated Pecorino cheese
1 lemon
1½ cups bread crumbs
⅓ cup olive oil
1 tbs. chopped sweet basil
Salt and pepper to taste

Mix bread crumbs with cheese, chopped basil, salt and pepper to taste.

Roll cutlets in bread crumbs; dip in egg; roll in bread crumbs.

Heat oil in skillet; brown cutlets quickly on both sides over high flame. Turn down flame; cover; continue frying about 20 minutes or until tender.

Serve very hot with lemon slices. Serves 4.

OSSI BUCHI ALLA MILANESE

VEAL SHANKS MILANESE

2 whole veal shanks
3 tbs. butter
3 tbs. olive oil
¼ cup chopped celery
1 medium carrot, chopped
1 medium onion, chopped
1 tsp. chopped parsley
2 tbs. tomato paste
1 cup dry sherry
Salt and pepper to taste

Have veal shanks sawed into 3-inch pieces. Melt butter and oil in deep saucepan; brown veal well on all sides (takes about 10 minutes). Add all chopped vegetables, salt and pepper to taste. Cover; simmer about 10 minutes or until carrots are soft.

Gradually add sherry into which tomato paste has been well blended. Stir occasionally to prevent burning or sticking. Cover; simmer over low flame for about 30 minutes or until veal is tender. While simmering, occasionally add small quantity of water if there is insufficient gravy.

Serve very hot with plain boiled rice. Serves 4.

ROLLINI DI VITELLA

VEAL ROLLETTES

1¼ lbs. rump of veal
4 ozs. prosciutto (Italian ham)
5 tbs. olive oil
2 cup canned tomatoes
1 large clove garlic, chopped
1 large onion, sliced
2 tbs. chopped parsley
Salt and pepper to taste

Have veal sliced very thinly and cut into 3-inch squares. Chop prosciutto; mix with chopped garlic, parsley, salt, and pepper. Place 1 heaping teaspoon of mixture and slice of onion on each square; roll carefully and tie with string or fasten with toothpicks.

Pour oil in hot skillet; brown rolls quickly on both sides about 5 minutes. Add tomatoes; cover; cook slowly for 30 minutes.

Serve very hot. Serves 4 to 6.

SCALOPPINE ALLA MARSALA

VEAL WITH MARSALA

1 lb. thin veal cutlets
1 sliced lemon
½ cup flour
½ cup marsala (sweet sherry)
⅛ lb. butter
Salt and pepper to taste

Have veal flattened and cut into 4-inch pieces. Roll veal in flour. Heat skillet; melt butter; brown cutlets quickly. Add marsala. Cover; simmer over low flame about 5 minutes or until meat is tender. Sprinkle with salt and pepper.

Serve very hot with lemon slices. Serves 4.

SPIEDINI ALLA GRIGLIA

BROILED VEAL ROLLS

1½ lbs. veal rump
4 ozs. prosciutto (Italian ham)
1 tbs. chopped parsley
1 clove garlic
Salt and pepper to taste
Pinch of rosemary
1 cup bread crumbs
3 tbs. grated Romano cheese
1 large onion, sliced
3 tbs. olive oil

Have veal sliced very thinly and cut into 3-inch squares. Chop prosciutto and garlic; mix thoroughly with grated Romano cheese, parsley, salt and pepper. Place 1 teaspoon of mixture in center of each veal square; roll carefully; tie with string or fasten with toothpicks.

Dip each roll in bread crumbs. Alternate 1 roll and 1

slice of onion on skewers until all are used. Brush with olive oil; sprinkle with rosemary. Place on broiler rack 5 inches below medium flame; broil about 5 minutes or until golden brown. Turn and brown other side 5 minutes or until veal is tender.

Serve very hot. Serves 4 to 6.

VITELLA CON RISO

VEAL WITH RICE

6 thin veal cutlets
¼ lb. Italian pork sausage
2 cups rice
1 thinly sliced onion
4 ozs. butter
2 tbs. olive oil
2 tbs. grated Romano cheese
1 cup canned tomatoes
2 tbs. chopped parsley
¼ cup hot water
1 qt. chicken broth
Salt and pepper to taste

Fry onion in 2 tablespoons of oil about 3 minutes or until soft. Add sausage cut up into small pieces; cook 5 minutes. Add washed rice; stir. Add tomatoes and parsley; stir; cook 5 minutes longer. Add chicken broth; lower flame; cover; cook 30 minutes longer, stirring frequently to prevent sticking. Add grated cheese; blend well to make a thick creamy mixture.

Fry cutlets quickly in butter about 10 minutes; add salt and pepper to taste. When golden brown, add ¼ cup of hot water to make brown gravy; simmer 5 minutes.

Arrange rice mixture on hot platter; place cutlets on top; pour gravy over this.

Serve very hot. Serves 6.

VITELLA CON PEPERONI

VEAL WITH PEPPERS

1½ lbs. veal rump
⅔ cup dry sauterne
5 tbs. olive oil
3 ozs. butter
1 large onion, sliced
4 large firm green peppers
1 No. 2 can tomatoes
Salt and pepper to taste

Have veal cut into 1½ inch cubes.

Clean, stem, and seed peppers; cut lengthwise into 1-inch strips.

Melt butter in skillet; brown veal about 10 minutes. Add salt and pepper, tomatoes; cover; simmer about 30 minutes over low flame.

Fry onions and peppers separately in hot oil for about 15 minutes or until tender. Stir to prevent burning. When done, mix with veal. Add sauterne; cover and simmer 15 minutes over very low flame.

Serve very hot. Serves 4 to 6.

UCCELLI SCAPPATI

VEAL BIRDS

1½ lbs. veal rump
4 slices bacon
Pinch of rosemary
Salt and pepper to taste

Have veal cut into 1½-inch cubes. Cut bacon in 1½-inch pieces.

Put skewer through center of each veal cube and piece of bacon. Alternate veal and bacon until skewer is filled. Sprinkle lightly with rosemary. Place on broiler rack about 6 inches below flame. Broil on each side about 6 minutes or until brown and tender. Then sprinkle with salt and pepper.

Serve very hot with pan gravy. Serves 4 to 6.

Miscellaneous Meats

CERVELLI IMPANATI

BREADED BRAINS

2 lbs. calves' brains
1 cup bread crumbs
1 tbs. grated Parmesan cheese
1 tbs. chopped parsley
¼ cup olive or peanut oil
Salt and pepper to taste

Wash brains thoroughly. Cover with cold water and parboil about 5 minutes. Remove from water; peel off all outer tissues. Cut into 3-inch serving pieces. Blend bread crumbs, parsley, cheese, salt, and pepper. Roll brains in this mixture. Pour oil in frying pan; heat. Fry brains about 5 minutes or until brown on both sides.

Serve very hot with green salad. Serves 4.

FEGATO CON FUNGHI ALLA GRIGLIA

BROILED LIVER AND MUSHROOMS

1 lb. calves' liver
4 tbs. olive oil
1 sliced onion
½ lb. mushrooms
1 tsp. fresh mint, chopped
2 tbs. wine vinegar
Salt and pepper to taste

Have liver sliced 1 inch thick and cut into 2-inch squares. Clean and remove stems from mushrooms.

Alternate a piece of liver, a mushroom cap, and slice of onion on 8 skewers until all ingredients are used.

Mix oil, vinegar, and mint thoroughly; brush liver and mushrooms on both sides. Place on broiler rack about 5 inches below flame. Broil three minutes on each side or until light brown. Salt and pepper to taste. Brush with remaining liquid; broil 1 minute longer and remove from skewers. If preferred, may be served on skewers.

Serve sizzling hot. Serves 4.

FEGATO CON VINO

LIVER WITH CLARET

1½ lbs. calves' liver
2 sliced onions
6 tbs. olive oil
½ cup claret
½ cup flour
Salt and pepper to taste

Have liver sliced ¾ inch thick. Sprinkle lightly with salt and pepper; roll in flour.

Pour oil in frying pan; heat. Brown onion about 3 minutes or until soft. Remove onion.

Fry liver quickly about 3 minutes on each side over high flame. Replace onion; add claret; turn flame very high for 1 minute. Remove from fire; serve immediately.

Serves 4.

POLPETTONE

MEAT LOAF

½ lb. chopped beef
½ lb. chopped lean pork
1 tbs. chopped parsley
4 tbs. olive oil
2 eggs
1 hard-boiled egg
3 tbs. grated Romano cheese
¼ lb. Mozzarella
Salt and pepper to taste

Mix meat, eggs, cheese, parsley, salt, and pepper thoroughly.

Pour 2 tablespoons of oil in bottom of small deep oblong baking dish. Put half of meat mixture in it. Slice Mozzarella and hard-boiled egg. Place layer of each over meat. Cover with balance of meat mixture to form a loaf. Pour 2 tablespoons of oil over loaf; bake in moderate oven about 25 minutes or until golden brown but not dry.

Slice and serve very hot. Serves 4.

POLPETTONE CON PATATE

MEAT LOAF WITH POTATO FILLING

1 lb. chopped lean beef
or
half beef and half veal
1 cup bread crumbs
1 tbs. chopped parsley
2 eggs
2 cups mashed potatoes
½ cup grated Parmesan cheese
½ cup water
½ lb. Mozzarella cheese
4 tbs. olive oil
1 small onion, chopped
Salt and pepper to taste

Blend 1 teaspoon of parsley with mashed potatoes.

Mix meat, bread crumbs, water, parsley, grated cheese, eggs, onions, salt, and pepper very thoroughly.

Brush a 10-inch Pyrex baking dish with 1 tablespoon of olive oil. Sprinkle lightly with 2 tablespoons of bread crumbs.

Place half of meat mixture in dish; alternate a layer of mashed potatoes and a layer of sliced Mozzarella. Top with balance of meat. Close edges firmly so potatoes do not show or ooze out. Brush with balance of oil. Bake 25 minutes in moderate oven until meat is golden brown but not dry.

Turn over on hot platter; slice and serve very hot. Serves 6.

POLPETTONE CON RICOTTA

MEAT LOAF WITH RICOTTA

1 lb. chopped lean beef
or
half beef and half veal
1 cup bread crumbs
3 eggs
4 tbs. olive oil
1½ tbs. chopped parsley
½ cup grated Romano cheese
½ cup water
1 small onion, chopped
¾ lb. ricotta (Italian cottage cheese)
Salt and pepper to taste

Mix meat, bread crumbs, water, 1 tablespoon of parsley, grated cheese, 2 eggs, onion, salt, and pepper very thoroughly.

Mix ricotta, 1 egg, ½ tablespoon of parsley, and pinch of salt until well blended.

Brush 10-inch Pyrex baking dish with 2 tablespoons of oil. Sprinkle lightly with 2 additional tablespoons of bread crumbs. Place half of meat mixture in dish. Spread ricotta mixture over this and top with balance of meat. Close edges firmly so ricotta does not ooze out. Brush with balance of oil. Bake about 25 minutes in hot oven or until meat is golden brown but not dry and ricotta is firm.

Turn over on heated platter. Slice and serve very hot. Serves 6.

ROGNONI AL VINO ROSSO

KIDNEYS WITH BURGUNDY

4 lamb kidneys
1 sliced onion
2 ozs. butter
1 pt. boiling water
2 tsp. chopped parsley or chopped sweet basil
½ cup burgundy
Salt and pepper to taste

Have all fat and outer membrane removed. Cut kidneys into ½-inch slices. Cover with cold salted water. Allow to stand for 1 hour. Drain. Clean kidneys well by placing in saucepan and pouring 1 pint of boiling water over them; drain thoroughly.

Melt butter in shallow saucepan. Place kidneys and onions in hot butter; cover; simmer for 20 minutes or until tender. Add salt and pepper to taste. Pour burgundy over kidneys; simmer 3 minutes. Sprinkle with parsley or basil.

Serve very hot. Serves 4.

SALSICCIA ALLA GRIGLIA

BROILED SAUSAGE

2½ lbs. Italian sausage

Place sausage on broiler rack 6 inches below medium flame. While broiling, prick in several places with fork to allow fat to escape. Broil 30 minutes or until well done and golden brown on all sides.

Serve very hot with sautéed green peppers and salad. Serves 4 to 6.

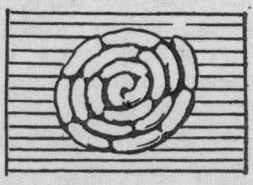

SALSICCIA CON VINO ROSSO

SAUSAGE WITH BURGUNDY

2½ lbs. Italian sausage
2 cups cold water
½ cup burgundy

Place cold water and sausage in skillet; boil briskly 3 minutes. Lower flame; prick sausage with fork, allowing fat to escape. Cook about 20 minutes or until all water evaporates and sausage is brown. Turn; brown other side 10 minutes or until well done. Gradually add burgundy; cover; simmer 5 minutes.

Serve very hot with salad. Serves 4 to 6.

TRIPPA MILANESE

TRIPE MILANESE

2 lbs. honeycomb tripe
2 cups boiled rice
1 cup water
½ cup tomato paste
2 ozs. butter
¼ cup grated Parmesan cheese
Salt and pepper to taste

Have tripe cut into 1-inch squares. Clean thoroughly by rinsing in cold water. Place tripe in 4 quarts of cold water in deep pot; cover; boil slowly about 2 hours or until tender. Drain.

Melt butter in saucepan. Add tripe; sauté for 5 minutes over low flame. Blend tomato paste in 1 cup of water; pour over tripe. Cover; simmer 30 minutes or until tripe is very tender. Blend in hot rice and cheese.

Serve very hot. Serves 4 to 6.

UMIDO DI CARNE

MEAT STEW

1 lb. lean beef
1 lb. lean lamb
4 tbs. olive oil
1 clove garlic
2 whole cloves
1 tbs. butter
½ cup burgundy
½ cup diced celery
1 No. 2 can tomatoes
3 sprigs parsley
3 large potatoes, quartered
1 chopped onion
Salt and pepper to taste

Have meat cut into 1½-inch cubes. Fry chopped onion and garlic in olive oil and butter about 5 minutes or until soft. Transfer to large saucepan. Add meat; brown well for about 10 minutes. Add burgundy gradually; stir to prevent burning. Add salt, pepper, tomatoes, celery, parsley, and cloves. Cover; cook for ½ hour over low flame. Add potatoes; continue cooking for about 20 minutes or until meat and potatoes are tender.

Serve very hot. Serves 6 to 8.

CHAPTER TEN

Vegetables and Salads

Vegetables

BROCCOLI CON OLIVE

BROCCOLI WITH OLIVES

Follow same recipe as for Broccoli Siciliana, but omit lemon and anchovy. Add ½ cup of chopped black Italian olives. Heat thoroughly and serve very hot.

BROCCOLI ALLA SICILIANA

BROCCOLI SICILIAN

1 bunch broccoli
1 clove garlic
3 filets of anchovy
4 tbs. olive oil
1 lemon
Salt and pepper to taste

Clean and wash broccoli. Cut into medium-sized pieces. Cook in rapidly boiling salted water for 10 minutes. Drain. Put olive oil, garlic, and anchovies (cut into small pieces) in saucepan. Heat thoroughly. Add broccoli and ¼ cup of warm water. Simmer for about 10 minutes or until tender. Flavor with lemon juice and serve very hot.
Serves 4.

CAPONATA ALA SICILIANA

DICED EGGPLANT SICILIAN

2 medium-sized eggplants
2 sliced onions
1 cup diced celery
1 No. 2 can strained tomatoes
2 ozs. capers (washed)
1 tbs. pine nuts
2 tbs. sugar
4 tbs. wine vinegar
½ cup olive oil
Salt and pepper to taste

Wash eggplants; dry with absorbent paper. Dice into 1-inch cubes. Fry in very hot oil about 10 minutes or until soft and slightly browned. Remove eggplant and put in large saucepan.

Fry onion in same oil about 3 minutes; add a little oil if necessary. When onions are golden brown, add tomatoes and celery; simmer about 15 minutes or until celery is tender. Add capers and nuts. Add this mixture to eggplant.

Dissolve sugar in vinegar; add salt and pepper to taste; heat slightly. Add to eggplant; cover; simmer about 20 minutes over very low flame. Stir occasionally to distribute flavor evenly. When done, place in bowl. Cool.

May be used as a side dish with meat or fowl; also as a sandwich filling or antipasto. Keeps for days in refrigerator. Serves 6 to 8.

CARCIOFI ARROSTITI

ROASTED ARTICHOKES

6 medium-sized artichokes
2 cloves garlic, chopped
6 tbs. olive oil
3 tbs. chopped parsley
½ cup water
Salt and pepper to taste

Remove outer leaves from artichokes. Cut off stems. Tap artichokes on table to spread leaves open. Wash; drain for few minutes.

Mix garlic, parsley, and a little salt and pepper (a

pinch of pepper and about ¼ teaspoon of salt). Divide mixture in 6 parts. Distribute one portion between the leaves of each artichoke. Then close leaves. Place upright in saucepan so they fit snugly. Add half of olive oil to bottom of pan; pour other half over the artichokes.

Cook over high flame for about 5 minutes. Watch carefully to prevent burning. Add water; lower flame a little; cook uncovered about 8 minutes or until water evaporates. Then add a little more water; cover pan; cook slowly about 20 minutes or until tender. Test by pulling outer leaf. If it comes off easily, artichokes are done.

Serve hot, as side dish. Serves 6.

CARCIOFI BOLLITI

BOILED ARTICHOKES

6 medium-sized artichokes
2 qts. water
1½ tsp. salt
1 slice lemon

Remove tough outer leaves from artichokes; cut off stems. Wash. Drain.

Place artichokes in 2 quarts of rapidly boiling salted water. Add lemon slice. Boil about 20 minutes or until tender. Test by pulling outer leaf. If it comes out easily, artichokes are done.

Serve hot or cold with French or Italian dressing. Serves 6.

CARCIOFI FRITTI

FRIED ARTICHOKES

12 boiled artichoke hearts (fresh or canned
2 eggs
6 tbs. olive oil
1 cup bread crumbs
1 tbs. chopped parsley
Salt and pepper to taste

Sprinkle artichoke hearts with salt and pepper. Mix parsley with bread crumbs. Beat eggs slightly.

Dip artichoke hearts in egg; roll in bread crumbs. Fry in hot olive oil about 3 minutes on each side or until golden brown.

Serve very hot. Serves 6.

CARCIOFI IMBOTTITI ALLA SICILIANA

STUFFED ARTICHOKES SICILIAN

4 large artichokes
1 cup bread crumbs
4 tbs. grated Caciocavallo cheese
4 chopped anchovy filets
2 cloves garlic, chopped
2 tbs. parsley, chopped
6 tbs. olive oil
Salt and pepper to taste

Cut off stems and about ½ inch tips of artichokes. Remove tough outer leaves. Wash carefully. Tap on table to spread leaves open. Shake out all water.

Mix thoroughly bread crumbs, grated cheese, chopped parsley, anchovies, garlic, salt, and pepper. Divide mixture into 4 parts; distribute one portion between the leaves of each artichoke. Then close. Place upright in saucepan to fit snugly. Pour 1 tablespoon of olive oil over each artichoke. Put remaining oil in saucepan. Add 1 cup of water. Cover tightly; cook slowly for ½ hour or until tender.

Test by pulling outer leaf. If it comes out easily, artichokes are done. Watch water carefully; if it evaporates, add a little more.

Serves 4.

CAVOLO IMBOTTITO

STUFFED CABBAGE

1 tender cabbage (about 3 lbs.)
1 cup chopped cooked spinach
1 tbs. chopped parsley
5 tbs. olive oil
½ lb. chopped cooked beef
½ cup grated Romano cheese
2 eggs
Salt and pepper to taste

Clean and boil whole cabbage in salted water for 5 minutes. Drain thoroughly.

Beat eggs slightly. Mix very thoroughly all other ingredients except oil.

Spread leaves carefully; insert some of stuffing in center of leaves until all is used. Then close by tying twine around cabbage to prevent stuffing from falling out.

Put in baking dish; add olive oil. Bake in medium oven for 25 minutes or until cabbage is tender. Add ½ cup of hot water if pan is dry.

Serves 6.

CICORIA FINA AGLIATA

DANDELION SAUTÉED WITH GARLIC

2 lbs. fresh dandelion greens
4 tbs. olive oil
2 cloves garlic, chopped
Salt and pepper to taste

Clean and wash dandelion greens thoroughly; cut in half.

Heat olive oil and garlic in saucepan. Add dandelion; salt and pepper to taste. Cook about 12 minutes or until tender. If too dry, add ¼ cup of hot water. Usually sufficient water is retained in vegetable; additional water is not necessary.

Serve very hot; enough for 4.

ESCAROLA IMBOTTITA

STUFFED ESCAROLE

2 medium heads escarole
5 ripe olives, chopped
4 filets of anchovy, chopped
1 tbs. pine nuts
1 tbs. seeded raisins
½ lb. chopped beef
½ cup bread crumbs
1 tbs. chopped parsley
5 tbs. olive oil
Salt and pepper to taste

Fry beef about 10 minutes or until slightly browned in 2 tablespoons of olive oil. Remove from fire. Add nuts, raisins, chopped olives, bread crumbs, chopped anchovy, parsley, very little salt and pepper. Mix thoroughly. If too dry, add 2 tablespoons of hot water.

Remove outer leaves from escarole. Wash heads thoroughly. Flatten them out. Place half of mixture in center. Close heads and tie with white twine so stuffing does not fall out.

Arrange in pan. Pour balance of oil over all. Cover tightly and cook over low flame about 20 minutes or until escarole is tender. Turn occasionally to avoid burning. If needed, add another tablespoon of olive oil.

May be used as an entrée. Serves 4.

ESCAROLA SAUTÉ

SAUTÉED ESCAROLE

2 lbs. escarole
1 clove garlic
4 tbs. olive oil
Salt and pepper to taste

Remove tough or faded outer leaves. Separate well. Wash thoroughly. Drain. Cut leaves in half. Heat oil in large saucepan; brown garlic, then remove. Add escarole and cook over medium flame for about 20 minutes or until tender. Salt and pepper to taste.

Serve very hot. Serves 4 to 6.

FAGIOLINI SAUTÉ

SAUTÉED STRING BEANS

1 lb. string beans
1 clove garlic
2 tbs. olive oil
Salt and pepper to taste

Clean and cut string beans in half. Wash again; drain. Cook in 1 quart of rapidly boiling salted water for about 20 minutes or until as tender as desired. Drain. Brown garlic in hot oil in saucepan for 2 minutes. Remove garlic. Add beans; sauté about 5 minutes.

Serve immediately when very hot. Serves 4 to 6.

FUNGHI ALLA PARMIGIANA

MUSHROOMS PARMESAN

1½ lbs. mushrooms
2 tbs. chopped parsley
2 cloves garlic, chopped
4 tbs. grated Parmesan cheese
¼ cup olive oil
½ tsp. orégano
¾ cup bread crumbs
Salt and pepper to taste

Clean mushrooms. Place in baking dish which has been brushed with 1 tablespoon of olive oil. Sprinkle with parsley, garlic, orégano, half of bread crumbs, and grated cheese. Add salt and pepper to taste. Pour balance of oil over this; sprinkle with balance of bread crumbs. Bake in moderate oven about 25 minutes or until mushrooms are tender. Add ¼ cup of hot water if mushrooms become too dry; bake 5 minutes longer.

Serve very hot. Serves 6.

FUNGHI IMBOTTITI

STUFFED MUSHROOMS

1 lb. large mushrooms
3 tbs. grated Parmesan cheese
1 clove garlic, chopped
1 small onion, chopped
1 cup bread crumbs
1 tbs. chopped parsley
2 tbs. melted butter
6 tbs. olive oil
Salt and pepper to taste

Clean and remove stems from mushrooms. Mix thoroughly bread crumbs, cheese, parsley, butter, garlic, onion, salt, and pepper. Fill mushroom caps.

Pour 2 tablespoons of oil in bottom of baking pan. Place mushrooms in pan, stuffed side up. Pour balance of oil equally over all mushrooms. Bake about 20 minutes in medium oven. When mushrooms are tender and tops are brown, remove from oven.

Serve very hot. Enough for 4 to 6.

MELENZANA FRITTA

FRIED EGGPLANT

1 large eggplant
2 ozs. grated Parmesan cheese
¾ cup peanut oil
2 tbs. chopped parsley
Salt and pepper to taste

Peel and cut eggplant crosswise into ½-inch slices. Place in bowl; cover with hot water and let stand for 5 minutes. Drain; dry with absorbent paper. Fry in hot oil about 3 minutes on each side or until soft and light brown. Sprinkle with salt and pepper to taste. Remove from frying pan. Arrange on heated platter; sprinkle with chopped parsley and grated cheese.

Serve very hot. Serves 4.

MELENZANA ALLA PARMIGIANA

EGGPLANT PARMESAN

1 large eggplant
2 cups bread crumbs
1 tbs. chopped parsley
2 cloves garlic, chopped
2 tbs. tomato paste
½ cup olive or peanut oil
½ lb. Mozzarella cheese
1 No. 2 can tomatoes
Salt and pepper to taste
½ cup grated Parmesan cheese

Blend tomato paste with tomatoes. Add 2 tablespoons of olive oil, a pinch of salt, and simmer in saucepan for 30 minutes.

Wash, dry, and slice eggplant crosswise into ½-inch slices. Place in bowl; cover with hot water and let stand for 5 minutes. Drain; dry with absorbent paper. Fry in hot oil about 3 minutes on each side or until soft and light brown. Sprinkle with salt and pepper to taste. Remove from pan.

Mix bread crumbs, cheese, parsley, garlic, a pinch of salt and pepper. Then place one layer of eggplant in bottom of baking dish; sprinkle with bread-crumb mixture; pour some tomato sauce over this. Alternate layers until all ingredients are used. Top with Mozzarella sliced thin. Bake for 10 minutes in moderate oven, or until Mozzarella turns slightly brown.

Serve very hot. Serves 4 to 6. May be used as an entrée.

MELENZANA ALLA GRIGLIA

BROILED EGGPLANT

1 large eggplant
1 cup Plain Tomato Sauce #1
½ cup Italian Salad Dressing
Salt and pepper to taste
2 ozs. grated Pecorino cheese

Peel and cut eggplant crosswise into ¾-inch slices. Marinate in dressing for 30 minutes. Broil under low flame for 5 minutes; turn and broil other side 5 minutes or until medium brown and soft. Arrange on Pyrex platter in layers; alternate hot tomato sauce and eggplant. Top with sauce. Sprinkle with grated cheese. Place under broiler for 2 minutes to brown cheese quickly.

Serves 4 to 6.

PEPERONI ARROSTITI

ROASTED PEPPERS

6 large firm green peppers
1 clove garlic, chopped
4 tbs. olive oil
1 tbs. vinegar
Salt and pepper to taste

Wash and dry peppers. Put on broiler rack 6 inches below medium flame. Broil about 10 minutes or until brown on both sides. Watch very carefully, turning frequently to prevent burning. When peppers are soft, remove and cool. Peel off brown skin; take out stems and seeds; cut lengthwise in 2-inch strips.

Mix oil, vinegar, and garlic very thoroughly. Add salt and pepper to taste. Place peppers in deep dish; pour mixture over them. Allow to marinate until ready to serve.

Serve cold with meat or fish. Serves 4.

PEPERONI FRITTI

FRIED PEPPERS

8 large firm green peppers
6 tbs. olive oil
1 clove garlic, halved
Salt and pepper to taste

Wash and dry peppers. Remove stems and seeds. Cut lengthwise into 1½-inch strips. Use large frying pan. Heat oil and garlic slightly. Add peppers, salt and pepper to taste. Fry over high flame for about 5 minutes. Watch carefully to prevent burning. Stir occasionally. When slightly brown, lower flame; cover; cook for about 15 minutes or until soft.

Serve hot with sausage or veal. Serves 6.

PEPERONI IMBOTTITI

STUFFED PEPPERS

6 large firm green peppers
3 filets of anchovy, chopped
5 tbs. olive oil
3 tbs. grated Romano cheese
1 tbs. chopped parsley
2 tbs. tomato paste
½ cup cooked chopped meat
½ cup boiled rice
½ cup bread crumbs
1 small onion, chopped
1 cup hot water
1 egg
Salt and pepper to taste

Blend tomato paste in hot water.

Wash peppers; remove stems and seeds. Combine all other ingredients except oil and tomato paste. Mix thoroughly. Stuff peppers.

Arrange in baking dish; pour oil over them. Bake in hot oven 15 minutes. Add blended tomato paste; continue baking for 15 minutes or until peppers are tender.

Serve very hot. Serves 6.

SPARAGI PARMIGIANA

ASPARAGUS PARMESAN

1 bunch fresh asparagus (about 2 lbs.)
⅛ lb. butter
Salt and pepper to taste
2 ozs. grated Parmesan cheese

Wash asparagus. Cut off tough ends; remove scales. Scrub stalks thoroughly or peel off outer skin. Cook in rapidly boiling salted water about 20 minutes or until partially tender. Place in baking dish. Melt butter; pour over asparagus; pepper lightly. Sprinkle generously with grated Parmesan cheese. Place in hot oven for about 10 minutes or until cheese turns slightly brown.

Serve very hot. Serves 4.

SPINACI AFFOGATI

STEAMED SPINACH

2 lbs. fresh spinach
4 tbs. olive oil
1 clove garlic
Salt and pepper to taste

Clean and wash spinach thoroughly. Heat olive oil and garlic in saucepan; add spinach, salt and pepper to taste. Cook about 12 minutes or until tender. If too dry, add ¼ cup of hot water. Usually sufficient water is retained in spinach; additional water is unnecessary.

Serves 6 to 8.

ZUCCHINI DOLCE E AGRO

SQUASH SWEET AND SOUR

6 medium-sized zucchini (Italian squash)
½ cup peanut oil
3 tbs. wine vinegar
1 tbs. sugar
1 tbs. chopped sweet basil
Salt and pepper to taste

Wash and scrape zucchini lightly. Cut into lengthwise slices about ⅜ inch thick. Fry in oil, about 3 minutes on each side or until slightly brown. Sprinkle with salt and pepper. When done, remove from frying pan and place in deep dish.

Mix thoroughly sugar and vinegar; add to remaining oil in frying pan. Boil slowly for 2 minutes. Pour this over the zucchini. Sprinkle with chopped basil.

Serve very hot or cold. Serves 4.

ZUCCHINI FRITTI

FRIED SQUASH

3 zucchini (about 2 in. in diameter, 8 in. long)
½ cup peanut oil
2 tbs. chopped parsley
2 ozs. grated Romano cheese
Salt and pepper to taste

Select 3 firm zucchini. Wash and scrape lightly. Cut crosswise into ½-inch slices. Fry in hot oil for about 3 minutes or until slightly brown and soft. Sprinkle with salt and pepper. When done, place on hot platter. Sprinkle each slice with chopped parsley and grated cheese.

Serve hot. Serves 6 to 8.

Salads

INSALATA D'ARANCIO E LIMONE

ORANGE AND LEMON SALAD

3 large lemons
1 head lettuce
½ tsp. chopped fresh mint
3 large oranges
4 tbs. olive oil
Salt and pepper to taste

Quarter unpeeled fruit or cut into small sections, as preferred. Place in salad bowl. Sprinkle lightly with mint, salt, and pepper. Pour olive oil over fruit and mix thoroughly. Place on lettuce leaves and serve.

Serves 6.

INSALATA DI CALAMAI

SQUID SALAD

2 lbs. squids
1 clove garlic
1 tbs. fresh mint, chopped
4 tbs. olive oil
Juice of 1 large lemon
Salt and pepper to taste

Have squids cleaned. Cut into small pieces about 2 inches long. Boil in 2 quarts of water about 30 minutes or until tender. Drain well. Add salt.

Blend ingredients well. Pour over squid. Marinate in cool place for several hours.

Serve cold on lettuce leaves. Serves 4 to 6.

INSALATA DI CICORIA FINA

DANDELION SALAD

1 lb. dandelion greens
4 tbs. olive oil
12 ripe olives
1 clove garlic
2 tbs. wine vinegar
Salt and pepper to taste

Remove undesirable leaves. Cut dandelion into 2-inch pieces; wash thoroughly in cold water. Drain; dry with absorbent paper. Chill in refrigerator about 10 minutes.

Rub wooden salad bowl with garlic; place dandelion in bowl. Pour olive oil and vinegar over leaves. Add salt and pepper to taste; add olives. Mix and toss thoroughly.

Serve immediately. Serves 4 to 6.

INSALATA D'ESCAROLA

ESCAROLE SALAD

1 medium head escarole
2 tbs. wine vinegar
6 tbs. olive oil
4 leaves fresh sweet basil, chopped
Salt and pepper to taste

Remove outside leaves. Wash thoroughly. Crisp in cold water for 15 minutes. Cut into 1-inch pieces. Drain; dry with absorbent paper.

Place escarole in salad bowl. Mix oil, vinegar, basil, salt, and pepper separately. Pour over salad. Toss and mix well.

Serves 4 to 6.

INSALATA DI FAGIOLINI

STRING BEAN SALAD

1 lb. string beans
1 clove garlic
2 qts. water
4 tbs. olive oil
2 tbs. vinegar
Salt and pepper to taste

Cut off tips of beans. Wash thoroughly. Place in rapidly boiling salted water. Cook about 20 minutes or until tender. Drain. Cut in half. Place in wooden salad bowl. Add oil, vinegar, garlic, salt and pepper to taste. Mix thoroughly.

May be served warm; otherwise chill in refrigerator 15 minutes. Serves 6.

INSALATA DI FINOCCHIO, POMODORO E CICORIA

FENNEL, TOMATO, AND CHICORY SALAD

1 head finocchio (fennel)
2 large firm tomatoes
1 small head chicory
6 tbs. olive oil
1 clove garlic
2 tbs. wine vinegar
Salt and pepper to taste

Remove outer leaves from finocchio and chicory. Wash thoroughly. Cut finocchio in thin slices. Cut chicory into 2-inch pieces. Wash thoroughly again. Dry with absorbent paper. Quarter tomatoes.

Rub large salad bowl with garlic. Add finocchio, chicory, tomatoes, salt and pepper to taste. Blend oil and vinegar separately; pour over salad. Toss and mix thoroughly. Chill in refrigerator for 5 minutes.

Serve on individual salad plates. Serves 6 to 8.

INSALATA DI LATTUGA ROMANA

ROMAINE SALAD

1 medium head romaine
6 tbs. olive oil
1 large sweet onion
2 tbs. wine vinegar
Salt and pepper to taste

Remove outside leaves from romaine. Wash thoroughly. Crisp in cold water for 15 minutes. Cut into 1-inch pieces. Drain; dry with absorbent paper. Slice onion.

Place romaine and onion in salad bowl. Mix oil, vinegar, salt, and pepper separately. Pour over salad. Toss and mix well.

Serves 4 to 6.

INSALATA MISTA

MIXED SALAD

½ head escarole
½ head chicory
¼ lb. dandelion greens
¼ medium-sized cucumber
6 tbs. olive oil
1 clove garlic
2 tbs. wine vinegar
Salt and pepper to taste

Peel and slice cucumber thinly. Remove outer leaves from all greens. Cut into 2-inch lengths. Wash thoroughly in cold water. Drain; dry.

Rub salad bowl with garlic. Put in mixed greens and sliced cucumber. Blend oil, vinegar, salt, and pepper and pour over salad. Toss and mix thoroughly.

Serves 6 to 8.

INSALATA DI PATATE E UOVA

POTATO AND EGG SALAD

4 large cold boiled potatoes
4 hard-boiled eggs
2 tsp. chopped parsley
6 tbs. olive oil
3 tbs. wine vinegar
½ cup chopped celery
Salt and pepper to taste

Cut potatoes into small cubes. Quarter eggs. Place in wooden salad bowl. Add celery and parsley. Blend oil and vinegar separately; add to salad. Sprinkle with salt and pepper. Thoroughly chill in refrigerator before serving.

Serves 6.

INSALATA DI POMODORO CON OREGANO

TOMATO SALAD WITH ORÉGANO DRESSING

4 large firm tomatoes
1 tbs. orégano
4 tbs. olive oil
Salt and pepper to taste

Wash, dry, and slice tomatoes; arrange on platter. Sprinkle with salt, pepper, and orégano. Pour olive oil over all. Chill in refrigerator.

Serves 4.

Salad Dressings

These dressings may be used with all green salads, including romaine, endive, escarole, chicory, and dandelion.

SWEET BASIL DRESSING

3 tbs. chopped sweet basil
4 tbs. wine vinegar
½ cup olive oil
1 clove garlic
Salt and pepper to taste

Blend all ingredients thoroughly. Place in jar; keep in cool place, *not cold*. Allow to stand several hours before using. Use as needed.

Excellent on all vegetable salads.

ITALIAN SALAD DRESSING

½ cup olive oil
¼ tsp. salt
1 clove garlic, halved
½ tsp. dry mustard
4 tbs. wine vinegar

Mix mustard, salt, and garlic thoroughly. Add vinegar; stir. Add oil; stir vigorously until all ingredients are well blended. Keep in jar in cold place. Use as needed. This may also be used as a basic recipe for other salad dressings.

GORGONZOLA CHEESE DRESSING

Use same ingredients and measurements as for Italian Salad Dressing. Add 2 ounces of crumbled Gorgonzola cheese. Stir thoroughly before using.

ROQUEFORT CHEESE DRESSING

Use same ingredients and measurements as for Italian Salad Dressing. Add 2 ounces of crumbled Roquefort cheese. Stir thoroughly before using.

CHAPTER ELEVEN

Game and Fowl

Game

CERVO ALLA MARIO

VENISON MARIO

4 lbs. venison
2 cups vinegar
4 cups cold water
1 cup sherry
4 strips salt pork or bacon
2 cloves
2 tbs. chopped parsley
2 cloves garlic
2 large onions
2 large carrots, diced
3 tbs. flour
Salt and pepper to taste

Blend vinegar and water; bring to a boil. Turn off flame; add carrots, garlic, parsley, clove, and 1 onion. Allow to cool. Put venison in this mixture. Let it marinate for 24 hours in a cold place.

Now prepare as follows:

Take venison out of mixture; dry it with absorbent paper. Sprinkle with salt and pepper. Rub with flour. Put 4 strips of salt pork or bacon over venison. Add whole onion and place in baking pan.

Brown venison on both sides in hot oven (this takes about 30 minutes). Then add all vegetables in which venison marinated; add a little of the liquid. Lower heat to moderate oven. Baste occasionally with liquid, using enough to make a gravy. Roast for about 1½ hours or until tender. Then add sherry; simmer slowly for 10 more minutes.

Serve very hot. Serves 6.

CONIGLIO FRITTO

FRIED RABBIT

1 rabbit (3 or 4 lbs.)
6 slices bacon
⅛ lb. butter
1 lemon
2 tbs. salt
Pinch of sage
Salt and pepper to taste

Have rabbit cleaned and cut into serving pieces. Place in deep dish. Cover with cold water; add 2 tablespoons salt. Let stand in cold place for about 4 hours. Remove. Wash in cold water; dry with absorbent paper.

Place bacon in skillet; brown slowly. Remove bacon; add butter and sage. Sprinkle rabbit lightly with pepper and very little salt to taste. Fry in hot pan for about 15 minutes or until golden brown. Lower flame; cover; continue frying about ½ hour or until tender.

Serve very hot with green salad and lemon slices. Serves 4 to 6.

CONIGLIO AL FORNO

ROASTED RABBIT

1 rabbit (3-4 lbs.)
2 sliced onions
6 slices bacon
1 cup hot water
1 tbs. salt
3 sliced carrots
2 tbs. olive oil
1 tsp. sage
Salt and pepper to taste

Have rabbit thoroughly cleaned. Wash in cold water. Place in deep pan. Cover with cold water; add 1 tablespoon of salt. Marinate 4 hours, then remove. Rinse with fresh water; dry with absorbent paper.

Sprinkle inside with sage, salt, and pepper. Insert 2 slices of bacon. Place 4 slices of bacon over rabbit. Place in baking pan. Pour in oil; arrange onions and carrots around rabbit. Roast in hot oven about 30 minutes or until brown on both sides. Baste occasionally. Lower flame. Add hot water; continue roasting about 30 minutes more or until tender. Baste occasionally.

Serve very hot with vegetables and salad. Serves 4 to 6.

CONIGLIO ALLA CACCIATORA #1

RABBIT HUNTER'S STYLE #1

1 rabbit (3 or 4 lbs.)
3 tbs. butter
2 tbs. olive oil
1 stalk celery, chopped
1 chopped carrot
1 medium onion, chopped
1 tsp. chopped parsley
2 tbs. salt
¾ cup dry sherry
1 tbs. tomato paste
Salt and pepper to taste

Have rabbit cleaned and cut into serving pieces. Place in deep dish. Cover with cold water. Add 2 tablespoons of salt; marinate for 4 hours. Dry with absorbent paper.

Melt butter and olive oil in hot skillet. Brown rabbit on all sides (about 10 minutes). Lower flame; add all chopped vegetables, salt and pepper to taste. Cover. Simmer about 10 minutes. Blend tomato paste and sherry; add gradually, stirring frequently to prevent burning. Cover; simmer over low flame about 45 minutes or until rabbit is tender. If necessary, add a small quantity of water to make additional gravy.

Serve very hot with boiled rice. Serves 4 to 6.

CONIGLIO ALLA CACCIATORA #2

RABBIT HUNTER'S STYLE #2

1 rabbit (4 or 5 lbs.)
1½ cups burgundy
4 tbs. olive oil
1 chopped onion
1 clove garlic
2 cups canned tomatoes
Pinch of rosemary
Salt and pepper to taste

Have rabbit cleaned and cut into small serving pieces. Place in bowl. Pour burgundy over it. Allow to marinate for 6 hours.

Heat olive oil in large saucepan. Add chopped onion; brown 3 minutes. Add rabbit, garlic, tomatoes, salt, and pepper. Cover; cook slowly 30 minutes. Gradually add the burgundy in which rabbit marinated. Add rosemary. Cook 20 minutes or until rabbit is tender.

Serve very hot. Serves 4 to 6.

UMIDO DI CONIGLIO

RABBIT STEW

1 rabbit (3-4 lbs.)
4 tbs. olive oil
2 medium onions, chopped
1 No. 2 can tomatoes
4 medium-sized potatoes
1 cup water
Salt and pepper to taste
1/8 tsp. crushed red pepper seeds

Have rabbit cleaned and cut into serving pieces. Place in enamel pot. Cover with water to which 2 tablespoons of salt have been added. Let it stand for 2 hours, then wash in cold running water and dry with absorbent paper.

Heat oil in pot. Sauté rabbit and onion for about 20 minutes. Season with salt and pepper; continue browning. Add tomatoes. Cover tightly; cook slowly for about 20 minutes. Add quartered potatoes and 1 cup of water. Continue cooking 1/2 hour longer or until rabbit and potatoes are tender.

Serves 4.

CONIGLIO DOLCE E AGRO

RABBIT SWEET AND SOUR

1 rabbit (3 or 4 lbs.)
2 tbs. tomato paste
2 ozs. olive oil
1 tbs. chopped salt pork
1 tbs. chopped parsley
1 tsp. sugar
1 tbs. wine vinegar
1 clove garlic, chopped
1 cup dry sauterne
2 tbs. raisins
2 tbs. pine nuts
1/4 tsp. crushed red pepper seeds
1/2 cup warm water
Salt and pepper to taste

Have rabbit cleaned and cut into small serving pieces.

Place olive oil and chopped salt pork in pot with parsley, garlic, and crushed pepper seeds. Add rabbit and brown well for about 30 minutes. Add salt and very little pepper, sugar, and vinegar; stir well. Pour 1/2 cup of sauterne over it. Cover; simmer 10 minutes. Add tomato paste blended in ½ cup of warm water. Lower flame; add nuts and raisins. Cover tightly; simmer about 20 minutes or until tender. Add remaining sauterne. Turn flame high; boil 1 minute.

Serve very hot. Serves 4 to 6.

Fowl

ANITRA AL COGNAC

BRANDIED DUCK

1 duck (6 lbs.)
2 large onions, chopped
2 tsp. chopped parsley
1 bay leaf
Pinch of thyme
½ lb. mushrooms
¼ cup olive oil
3 jiggers cognac
1 clove garlic
1 pint claret
Salt and pepper to taste

Have duck cleaned and cut into serving pieces. Sprinkle lightly with salt and pepper. Put in deep enamel dish. Add onions, parsley, bay leaf, thyme, garlic, cognac, and claret. Marinate for 4 hours.

Put oil in earthenware casserole; heat over high flame. Brown duck in oil for about 12 minutes. Then add liquid and sliced mushrooms. Cover; simmer over low flame for 1 hour or until duck is tender.

Serve hot. Enough for 4 to 6.

FAGIANO O CONIGLIO SELVAGGIO

PHEASANT OR WILD RABBIT

Use about 4 pounds of pheasant or wild rabbit and follow the same recipe and directions as for Venison Mario.

While roasting, add bay leaf to gravy for additional flavor.

PERNICE AL FORNO

ROASTED PARTRIDGE

1 partridge (about 4 lbs.)
6 slices bacon
3 ozs. butter
½ tsp. sage
Salt and pepper to taste

Wash partridge thoroughly; wipe well with damp cloth. Rub inside and outside with butter. Sprinkle inside with sage. Arrange bacon strips over partridge. Place in roasting pan. Roast in hot oven 20 minutes or until golden brown. Baste occasionally. Add ½ cup of hot water to bottom of pan if dry. Lower flame; sprinkle with salt and pepper; roast 25 minutes longer or until tender. Continue basting. Remove from oven. Use pan gravy.

Serve very hot. Serves 4.

PICCIONE SAUTÉ

PIGEON SAUTÉ

4 plump pigeons
4 tbs. olive oil
1 tsp. sage
1 tsp. chopped parsley
½ cup hot water
⅛ lb. butter
1 lemon slice
4 slices bacon
Salt and pepper to taste

Have pigeons cleaned thoroughly. Brush with olive oil. Insert little butter and pinch of sage inside each pigeon. Sprinkle outside lightly with salt and pepper.

Brown bacon slightly in skillet over low flame. Remove. Brown pigeons about 5 minutes on each side. Lower flame; replace bacon. Add hot water, parsley, and lemon. Cover; simmer for 10 minutes or until tender.

Serve very hot. Serves 4.

PICCIONI RIPIENI

STUFFED PIGEONS

4 plump pigeons
1 cup bread crumbs
¼ tsp. marjoram
1 chopped onion
1 tsp. chopped parsley
½ cup hot water
¼ cup Romano cheese
1 sliced lemon
2 tbs. butter
6 tbs. olive oil
4 slices bacon
Salt and pepper to taste

Have pigeons thoroughly cleaned and washed. Cut off wing tips. Brush with olive oil; sprinkle with salt and pepper to taste.

Mix all ingredients except bacon; blend thoroughly. Stuff pigeons. Skewer them. Wrap slice of bacon around each. Pour balance of oil in baking dish. Place pigeons in it. Roast in medium oven about 20 minutes or until brown and tender. Baste occasionally. Add ½ cup of hot water. Roast 10 minutes more.

Serve hot with lemon slices and green salad. Serves 4.

POLLO AL BURRO

BUTTERED CHICKEN

1 roasting chicken (3½-4 lbs.)
2 tbs. olive oil
2 cloves garlic
¼ lb. butter
3 sprigs parsley
Salt and pepper to taste

Wash and dry chicken thoroughly. Rub inside with half of butter. Insert parsley, 1 clove of garlic. Sprinkle with salt and pepper. Sew or skewer opening.

Rub outside of chicken with salt and balance of butter. Put 1 clove of garlic, oil, and chicken in baking pan. Roast in moderate oven for about 1 hour or until golden brown and tender. Baste occasionally with pan juice.

Cut into serving pieces; serve very hot. Serves 4.

If you wish to serve whole pan-browned potatoes, peel 8 small ones. After chicken has roasted for about 30 minutes, add the potatoes; turn occasionally to brown. If pan is dry, add 1 tablespoon of oil and ½ cup of water. Potatoes will be done in about 30 minutes.

POLLO ALLA CACCIATORA #1

CHICKEN HUNTER'S STYLE #1

1 frying chicken (4 lbs.)
4 small onions
5 tbs. olive oil
½ cup flour
1 clove garlic, chopped
1 cup canned tomatoes
1 cup sliced mushrooms
1 large green pepper
Salt and pepper to taste

Cut chicken into serving pieces. Season with salt and pepper; roll lightly in flour. Heat oil in skillet and brown chicken on all sides about 10 minutes.

Stem, seed, and slice green pepper lengthwise. Mix with onions, garlic, and tomatoes; add mixture to chicken. Cover; simmer slowly for 40 minutes. Add mushrooms; simmer 15 minutes or until mushrooms and chicken are tender.

Serve very hot. Serves 4 to 6.

POLLO ALLA CACCIATORA #2

CHICKEN HUNTER'S STYLE #2

1 roasting chicken (4 lbs.)
2 tbs. butter
3 tbs. olive oil
1 stalk celery, chopped
1 medium carrot, chopped
1 medium onion, chopped
1 tsp. chopped parsley
1 tbs. tomato paste
¾ cup dry sherry
Salt and pepper to taste

Have chicken cleaned and cut into serving pieces.

Melt butter and olive oil in hot skillet. Brown chicken on each side about 5 minutes. Add all chopped vegetables, salt and pepper to taste. Simmer about 10 minutes or until vegetables are partially tender. Gradually add sherry into which tomato paste has been well blended. Cover.

Stir occasionally to prevent sticking. Simmer about 30 minutes or until chicken is tender. If these is insufficient gravy, add small quantity of water from time to time.

Serve very hot. Serves 4 to 6.

POLLO COLLA MARSALA

CHICKEN WITH MARSALA

1 roasting chicken (4 lbs.)
4 ozs. butter
1 sliced onion
¼ cup water
½ cup marsala (heavy sweet sherry)
Salt and pepper to taste

Have chicken cleaned and cut into serving pieces. Sprinkle lightly with salt and pepper to taste. Melt butter in skillet. When very hot, add chicken. Brown on both sides about 5 minutes. Add onion; brown 2 minutes. Lower flame; add water; cover; simmer about 20 minutes or until tender. Add marsala; simmer for 10 minutes. If necessary, add small quantity of water.

Serve very hot. Serves 4 generous portions.

POLLO CON FUNGHI

CHICKEN WITH MUSHROOMS

1 broiler (3-4 lbs.)
1 lb. fresh mushrooms
2 cloves garlic
1 large onion, sliced
6 tbs. olive oil
1 tbs. butter
½ cup sherry
Salt and pepper to taste

Cut chicken into serving pieces; wash and dry thoroughly. Sprinkle lightly with salt and pepper to taste.

Heat butter in skillet; add garlic and 4 tablespoons of oil. Brown chicken on both sides about 10 minutes. Lower flame; cover; continue cooking for 25 minutes.

Sauté sliced onion in 2 tablespoons of olive oil in separate saucepan for 5 minutes. Add cleaned, sliced mushrooms and 2 tablespoons of water. Simmer 15 minutes; add to chicken. Cover. Simmer chicken and mushrooms

15 minutes longer. Pour in ½ cup sherry; boil up quickly for 1 minute.

Serve very hot. Serves 4.

POLLO CON ROSAMARINA

CHICKEN WITH ROSEMARY

1 broiler (3-4 lbs.)
3 tbs. olive oil
1 tbs. butter
1 tsp. rosemary
2 cloves garlic
¼ cup water
Salt and pepper to taste

Have chicken cleaned and cut into serving pieces. Wash and dry thoroughly. Sprinkle lightly with salt and pepper to taste.

Melt butter in skillet. Add oil and garlic; heat. Brown chicken on both sides about 10 minutes. Sprinkle with rosemary. Gradually add a little water; cover; simmer over low flame about 25 minutes or until tender. Gradually add more water, if necessary, to prevent burning.

Serve very hot. Serves 4.

POLLO IMBOTTITO

STUFFED CHICKEN

1 roasting chicken (4-5 lbs.)
1 tbs. olive oil
¼ lb. butter
Salt and pepper to taste

Stuffing:

½ cup boiled rice
½ cup bread crumbs
1 egg
2 strips chopped prosciutto (Italian ham)
2 tbs. olive oil
¼ tsp. marjoram
1 clove garlic, chopped
2 tsp. chopped parsley
3 tbs. grated Romano cheese
Salt and pepper to taste

Wash and dry chicken thoroughly. Rub outside with half of butter and 1 tablespoon of olive oil. Salt and pepper to taste.

Mix all stuffing ingredients thoroughly. If dry, add 1 tablespoon of milk. Stuff chicken; sew or skewer together to prevent stuffing from falling out. Place chicken and balance of butter in roasting pan. Brown on both sides in very hot oven. If pan is too dry, add ¼ cup of hot water to keep moist. After 30 minutes, lower flame; continue roasting in moderate oven 1 hour longer or until chicken is tender. Baste occasionally.

Serves 6.

POLLO IN UMIDO

CHICKEN STEW

1 roasting chicken (4 lbs.)
2 sliced onions
1 cup canned tomatoes
4 tbs. olive oil
Pinch of marjoram
2 cups hot water
1 cup boiled fresh peas
1 tbs. chopped parsley
1 cup diced potatoes
Salt and pepper to taste

Have chicken cleaned and cut into serving pieces. Wash and dry thoroughly.

Brown chicken slightly in hot oil for about 10 minutes. Sprinkle lightly with salt and pepper. Add onion; simmer for 5 minutes. Then add parsley, marjoram, tomatoes and 1 cup of hot water. Cover; simmer about 30 minutes. Add potatoes and peas. Continue cooking for ½ hour or until chicken and potatoes are tender. If stew has absorbed too much liquid, gradually add a little hot water to make sufficient gravy.

Serves 4 to 6.

POLLO OREGANATO

CHICKEN ORÉGANO

1 broiler (about 4 lbs.)
1 tsp. chopped parsley
2 tsp. orégano
⅓ cup olive oil
¼ cup lemon juice
1 clove garlic, chopped
Salt and pepper to taste

Have broiler cleaned and quartered. Sprinkle lightly with salt and pepper.

Mix olive oil, orégano, lemon juice, garlic, and parsley thoroughly. Brush chicken generously with this mixture. Place on broiler rack about 6 inches beneath high flame. Broil about 20 minutes on each side or until brown and tender. Brush occasionally with liquid to prevent dryness. When done, pour balance of liquid over chicken and serve very hot.

Serves 4.

QUAGLIA ALLA GRIGLIA

BROILED QUAIL

6 quail
6 slices bacon
6 tsp. butter
Salt and pepper to taste

Have quail cleaned thoroughly. Wash. Dry with damp cloth. Sprinkle inside with salt and pepper; place 1 teaspoon of butter in each bird. Wrap slice of bacon around each.

Place quail on broiler rack about 6 inches below medium flame. Broil about 10 minutes on each side or until golden brown and tender.

Serve very hot on toast. Serves 6.

CHAPTER TWELVE

Desserts

CAFFE ESPRESSO

BLACK COFFEE

6 tbs. Italian-roasted coffee
6 cups water
Peel of 1 lemon
or
12 tsp. cognac
1 Caffettiera (Italian coffee maker)

Use coffee which has been roasted very black in the Italian manner. Have it pulverized. In American stores it is identified as "French-roasted" but is called Italian-roasted in all Italian stores. In some sections of the country pulverized Italian coffee may be purchased in cans.

An Italian coffee maker called a "Caffettiera" may be purchased in any Italian store which carries pottery and hardware.

The "Caffettiera" has two sections: the lower part holds a strainer-top container for the coffee; the upper has an inverted spout.

Remove top part; lift out strainer-top container from the lower part; fill with coffee. Place water in bottom section. Replace container. Cover with top section.

Place over high flame. When steam escapes from tiny opening in lower section, the water is boiling. Grasp handles firmly; remove from fire and reverse the entire "Caffettiera" quickly. The boiling water drips through the coffee in a few moments and the Caffe Espresso is ready to serve.

To keep very hot, allow to stand over low flame. Never reheat.

SECTIONS OF COFFEE-MAKER

BOILING POSITION

POSITION FOR DRIPPING

SERVING POSITION

May be served in 4-ounce glasses with a twist of lemon peel, or in a demitasse with cognac. Serves 12.

AMARETTI

MACAROONS

½ lb. sugar
¼ lb. shelled blanched almonds
¼ tsp. almond extract
2 egg whites

Chop and pulverize almonds; mix thoroughly with half of sugar and extract.

Beat eggwhites until very stiff. Add balance of sugar; beat again. Add almond mixture; mix thoroughly. Shape into balls or cookies about 2 inches in diameter. Place on greased cookie pan about 1 inch apart. Bake in moderate oven about 5 minutes or until light brown.

Makes about 1 dozen, depending upon size desired.

BISCOTTI AL'ANICI

AUNT LENA'S ANISE SLICES

6 eggs
1 lb. flour
6 drops anise oil (purchased at drugstore)
½ lb. butter or shortening
½ cup sugar
1 tsp. baking powder
½ teaspoon salt

Beat 5 eggs with salt; add sugar; blend thoroughly.

Sift flour and baking powder; add to eggs and sugar mixture. Add anise oil (which may be purchased at a drugstore), softened butter or shortening; mix well. Knead until dough is smooth and manageable. Then roll dough into oblong loaf 5 inches broad and about ¾ inch thick. Brush with 1 beaten egg; sprinkle with sugar; cut into 1-inch slices.

Place slices in greased baking pan; bake for 15 minutes in moderate oven, or until light brown.

Enough for 2½ dozen slices. An unusual flavor!

BISCOTTI DI ZIA LENA

AUNT LENA'S COOKIES

3 cups flour
2 tps. baking powder
2 eggs
½ cup chopped walnuts
½ cup shortening
½ cup sugar
¼ cup milk
½ tsp. cinnamon
Pinch of salt

Mix all dry ingredients except nuts; blend shortening with hands; beat eggs and add to mixture. Add milk gradually and form into a ball. Knead and mold dough until smooth. Roll small pieces into 3-inch oblong shapes. Sprinkle tops with chopped nuts. Bake in moderate oven about 15 minutes or until golden brown.

Makes about 3 dozen, depending upon size desired.

CASSATA ALLA SICILIANA

CREAM TART SICILIAN

1 spongecake (10-12 in. in diameter)
½ cup sugar
¼ lb. glazed mixed fruit
1½ lbs. ricotta (Italian cottage cheese)
2 squares bitter chocolate, chopped
2 tsp. almond extract

Strain ricotta through wire sieve to refine. Add sugar; mix thoroughly. Add chocolate and almond extract; blend until custard-like consistency is obtained. Set aside in cold place until ready to use.

Cut plain spongecake in 3 layers. Put bottom layer in large round dish. Spread about ½ inch thick with filling. Top this with another layer of cake, then another ½ inch of the filling. Top layer should be spongecake. Set in refrigerator until this frosting is ready:

1 egg white
1 tsp. almond extract
1½ cups sifted confectioners' sugar
½ tsp. lemon juice

Gradually mix 1 cup of sugar with egg white; beat with spoon until smooth. Add flavoring and lemon juice; blend with more sugar (about ½ cup) until thick enough to spread.

Cover sides and top of Cassata evenly. Place cherry in center. Distribute glazed fruit on top to form an attractive design. Sprinkle with nuts and citron if desired.

Serves 10 to 12.

CASSATELLE ALLA SICILIANA

SICILIAN CREAM TARTLETS

Dough:

1 lb. flour
1 egg
4 tbs. tepid water
2 tbs. sugar
2 tbs. claret
3 tbs. shortening
1 tsp. vanilla
2 tsp. baking powder
Pinch of salt

Dissolve sugar in tepid water. Mix all other ingredients except claret. Add water slowly. Knead well. While dough is stiff, gradually add wine. Continue kneading until dough can be rolled out easily. Place in bowl. Set aside in cool place for 30 minutes.

In the meantime, prepare this cream filling:

1 lb. ricotta (Italian cottage cheese)
1 square bitter chocolate, chopped
1 tbs. chopped citron
1 tsp. almond flavor
4 tbs. sugar
2 tbs. grated orange rind
1 tsp. grated lemon rind
1 pt. peanut oil

Blend all ingredients, except peanut oil, thoroughly until a custard-like consistency is obtained. If too dry, add a little milk and continue blending. Place in bowl. Set in refrigerator until used.

Cut dough into 3 sections. Roll out on lightly floured board until very thin. Cut dough into disks about 3 inches in diameter. Fry in very deep hot oil 1 minute or until golden brown on both sides. Drain on brown paper. Set aside to cool.

When disks are cold, put one in palm of hand and spread with a tablespoon of cream filling; top with another disk. This forms the tartlet. Repeat until all are used. Sprinkle with powdered sugar.

Makes about 2 dozen. A real treat for the holidays.

FARFALLETTE DOLCI

SWEET BOWKNOTS

6 eggs
3 tbs. granulated sugar
3 cups flour
½ tsp. orange flavor
½ cup powdered sugar
¼ tsp. salt
2 tbs. butter
1 tsp. almond flavor
3 cups peanut oil

Beat eggs lightly; add granulated sugar, salt, and flavoring; blend thoroughly.

Place flour on board; cut in butter; add egg mixture. Knead until smooth ball is obtained. If dough is too soft, gradually add a little flour to make firm but not hard. Set aside for 30 minutes.

Then cut dough in 4 sections. Roll on well-floured board until wafer-thin. Cut with pastry cutter into strips 6 inches long by ¾ inch wide. Tie in individual bowknots. Fry bows about 3 minutes or until light brown in deep hot peanut oil. Drain on absorbent paper; cool; sprinkle with powdered sugar.

Makes about 6 to 7 dozen bowknots.

LA CREMA

DE LUXE CREAM CAKE

4 eggs
4 tbs. sugar
4 cups milk
4 tbs. cornstarch
Rind of one lemon, cut in one piece
2 lbs. plain poundcake
1 oz. bittersweet chocolate, chopped
1 tsp. almond extract
1 maraschino cherry
2 tbs. diced citron

Blend cornstarch in ½ cup milk. Combine with rest of milk, eggs, sugar, and lemon rind. Blend thoroughly in saucepan.

Cook over slow fire about 10 minutes; stir constantly until it comes to a boil. Remove from fire immediately; take out lemon rind; add almond extract. Cool.

Slice poundcake in ¼-in thick slices. Arrange 1 layer of cake on bottom of 10-inch pie plate; pour some of mixture (about ½ inch thick) over this. Alternate until all cake and mixture is used. The top layer should be cream. Place in refrigerator 4 to 5 hours or until ready to serve. Then sprinkle chopped chocolate and citron over top with a cherry in center for color.

Serves 10 to 12.

PALLOTTOLE D'ARANCI

ORANGE BALLS

½ lb. fresh orange peels
¼ lb. chopped mixed nuts
½ lb. sugar
1 tsp. vanilla

Use about six large California oranges. Peel thickly with sharp knife. Soak peels in cold water for 24 hours. Drain. Weigh peels. Place in saucepan; cover with cold water; bring to a boil. Cook about 10 minutes or until soft; drain.

Chop orange peels fine; mix with sugar; cook slowly over low flame about 10 minutes or until a small quantity dropped into cold water forms a soft ball. Add vanilla; blend thoroughly. Remove from fire; cool; shape into small balls about size of small walnut. Roll in sugar; dip in finely chopped nuts. Something different!

PANE DI SPAGNA

SPONGE CAKE

8 egg yolks
8 egg whites
2 tsp. grated lemon rind
2 tsp. almond extract
1⅓ cups flour
1¼ cups sugar
1½ tbs. water
¼ tsp. salt

Use large mixing bowl. Sift ½ cup of sugar with flour several times to blend well. Place egg yolks, water, and grated lemon rind in bowl. Beat lightly; add almond extract. Gradually sift flour very lightly over beaten egg yolks. Fold in gently.

Place egg whites in another mixing bowl and beat until foamy. Add salt and balance of sugar; beat until stiff. Gently fold the stiff egg whites into flour mixture. Pour into 10- or 12-inch ungreased cake pan. Bake in moderate oven 45 minutes, or until cake separates from sides of pan. Be careful not to jar cake while baking, as it may become heavy.

When cake is done, invert pan on wire rack for about 1 hour or until cold. Remove from pan.

PERE RIPIENE ALLA MILANESE

STUFFED PEARS MILANESE

6 large firm pears
3 ozs. powdered sugar
4 maraschino cherries
¼ lb. shelled toasted almonds
¼ tsp. almond extract
½ cup dry sherry

Wash pears. Cut in half lengthwise; scoop out cores. Chop cherries very fine. Grind almonds until almost mealy; add extract. Blend very thoroughly all ingredients except sherry.

Fill pear halves with this mixture. Place in baking dish. Pour sherry over pears; bake in medium oven about 15 minutes, or until pears are done but not too soft.

Serve either very hot or cooled, as preferred. Serves 6 to 8.

PESCA CON VINO ROSSO

PEACH WITH BURGUNDY

1 large ripe peach
2 ozs. burgundy (chilled)

Peel one large ripe peach; slice lengthwise. Place in large sherbet glass; pour 2 ounces of burgundy over peach.

Serve immediately. Serves 1.

PESCHE IMBOTTITE ALLA MANDORLA

PEACHES STUFFED WITH ALMONDS

6 large firm fresh peaches
or
12 halves canned peaches
1 tbs. chopped glazed orange peel or citron
2 ozs. shelled toasted almonds
3 ozs. powdered sugar
½ cup dry sherry

Peel, pit, and halve fresh peaches. Chop and pulverize almonds until mealy; add half the sugar; mix thoroughly. Add citron or orange peel; blend. Then fill peach halves. Place in baking pan. Sprinkle with balance of sugar; pour in sherry. Bake in moderate oven 10 minutes.

Serve warm. Serves 6.

PASTICCIO

FLAKY PIE CRUST

2½ cups flour
⅓ cup ice water
1 tsp. almond extract
¾ tsp. salt
1 cup butter or shortening

Sift together flour and salt. Gently blend in shortening; add flavoring; gradually add sufficient water to hold ingredients together. Gently form a smooth ball. Cut in half.

Roll out dough in circular piece about ⅛ inch thick on lightly floured board.

Sufficient for a 2-crust 8- or 9-inch pie.

PIGNOLATA-STRUFOLI

PINE-NUT CLUSTERS

2 eggs
2 cups flour
2 cups peanut oil
¼ tsp. salt
½ cup honey
2 tbs. pine nuts
1 tbs. colored candied confetti
½ cup sugar

Place 1 cup of flour on board; break in eggs; add salt; knead together gently. Gradually add enough flour to make medium-soft, easily molded dough. Texture becomes soft with kneading. When very smooth, cut in half.

Roll out dough in circular piece about ¼ inch thick on lightly floured board. Cut into strips about ¼ inch wide. Mold each strip gently to resemble a small rope about 10 inches long (on lightly floured board). Cut into tiny pieces about ¼ inch. Each bit of dough resembles a grape or small marble. Distribute on lightly floured board to prevent sticking.

Heat oil in deep saucepan. When very hot, gradually add small pieces (about 6 tablespoons at a time), stirring constantly with wooden spoon. Brown lightly for 1 or 2 minutes; remove with perforated spoon. Drain on absorbent paper.

Blend sugar and honey in large deep skillet; stir constantly. Heat about 5 minutes over low flame. When very smooth, add all browned pieces, stirring constantly with wooden spoon. When covered with honey mixture, remove quickly; place on 2 large platters. Mold with spoon into desired forms (as bunches of grapes or small clusters). Top each form with pine nuts; sprinkle with colored confetti. Allow to cool.

Serve by breaking off individual pieces with cake fork. Pignolata-Strufoli keeps fresh for 2 weeks when placed in cakebox. Serves 8 to 10.

SFINGE DI SAN GIUSEPPE

ST. JOSEPH'S CREAM PUFFS

¼ lb. butter
¼ tsp. salt
1 cup flour
1 cup water
18 maraschino cherries
4 eggs
1 tbs. sugar
1 tbs. grated lemon rind
1 tsp. grated orange rind
½ cup glazed orange peel

Place water and butter in saucepan; bring to a boil. Add flour and salt; keep stirring until mixture leaves sides of pan or forms a ball in the center. Remove from stove and cool. Add eggs one at a time, beating each in thoroughly.

Add sugar, orange peel, and lemon rind; mix well. Drop by tablespoon on cooky pan, placing the puffs about 3 inches apart, or put in muffin tins.

Heat oven to 400 degrees and bake 10 minutes. Then reduce temperature to 350 and bake about ½ hour or until light brown. Remove from oven. Open puffs immediately to allow steam to escape. (Puffs should be opened through center top.) Cool. Fill with Ricotta Filling; top with a cherry and two thin slices of glazed orange peel. (A plain custard filling may be substituted if desired.)

Ricotta Filling:

1 lb. ricotta (Italian cottage cheese)
2 tbs. grated chocolate
1 tbs. grated orange rind
Sugar to taste
3 tbs. milk
2 tsp. almond extract

Blend all ingredients thoroughly. Use milk sparingly, and only if needed to make smooth custard-like mixture. Put in refrigerator until used.

Recipe makes approximately 18 cream puffs.

SAVOIARDI

LADY FINGERS

2 cups sifted flour
1 cup sugar
4 eggs
2 tsp. baking powder
1 tbs. almond extract
Pinch of salt

Beat sugar and eggs until thoroughly blended and cream-colored. Mix flour, salt, and baking powder; sift slowly into egg mixture. Keep beating until smooth, creamy consistency is obtained. (Use of an electric mixer is advisable since it reduces work and will produce a smoother batter.)

Butter cooky pans generously and sprinkle with a little flour. Drop batter by spoonfuls, shaping it about 3 inches long and 1 inch wide. Place about 1½ inches apart, as they spread when baking. Bake in medium oven about 10 minutes or until light brown.

Enough for 3 dozen, depending upon size and shape.

SPUMONI

ITALIAN ICE CREAM

Mixture # 1 Outside Custard:

1 qt. milk
4 tbs. cornstarch
1¼ cups sugar
2 tbs. chopped almonds
5 egg yolks
⅛ tsp. salt

Mixture # 2 Cream Filling:

½ pt. heavy cream
½ cup sugar
6 maraschino cherries
2 tbs. candied orange peel

Prepare Mixture #1 as follows:

Blend cornstarch in ½ cup of milk. Combine with balance of milk, egg yolks, and sugar. Blend thoroughly in deep saucepan.

Cook very slowly over hot water; stir constantly, about 10 minutes or until mixture thickens and comes to a boil. Remove from fire immediately. Stir in chopped almonds. Cool.

Pour into freezing tray of refrigerator. When firm but not hard, remove from tray.

While Mixture #1 is freezing, prepare Mixture #2 as follows:

Pour cream in deep chilled mixing bowl; whip until firm. Add sugar; whip until very thick. Chop maraschino cherries and orange peel very fine; blend into whipped cream. Place bowl in refrigerator to keep cold and stiff while preparing molds.

Spumoni molds are always made to order. If unable to purchase them, use 10 to 12 individual aluminum, covered jello molds.

Chill molds before using.

Remove Mixture #1 (outside custard) from freezing tray. Line individual molds with 1-inch thickness of this partially frozen custard. Leave hollow in center of mold. Fill hollow with Mixture #2 (cream filling). Cover with Mixture #1. Cover molds. If molds are without covers, protect spumoni by covering with 2 thicknesses of heavy waxed paper.

Place individual molds in freezing compartment of refrigerator at degree set for freezing.

Makes enough spumoni to serve 10 to 12.

TORTA DI PISTACCHIO

PISTACHIO PIE

Pastry:

2 cups flour
1 egg
¼ tsp. salt
¼ lb. butter
½ cup sugar
2 tbs. sherry

Sift together flour, sugar, and salt. Beat egg lightly. Blend all ingredients with butter in deep bowl. Gradually add enough sherry to form firm pastry. Roll in circular piece about ⅛ inch thick to fit 9- or 10-inch pie plate. Butter plate before placing pastry in it. For an even fluted standing rim, pinch edges of pastry. Cut balance of pastry in strips ½ inch wide to use as a crisscross (lattice) top.

Pistachio Filling:

1 pt. sweet milk
2 eggs
4 ozs. pistachio nuts
2 ozs. granulated sugar
¾ cup whole-wheat flour
¼ tsp. nutmeg
1 tbs. powdered sugar
Pinch of salt

Chop nuts medium-fine. Place flour in deep saucepan. Gradually blend in milk until mixture is very smooth. Add granulated sugar, beaten eggs, salt, and nutmeg. Blend thoroughly. Place over medium flame; stir constantly to prevent lumping and sticking; bring to a boil. Lower flame; cook for 10 minutes; continue stirring. Gradually add nuts. Continue stirring vigorously until all is a well-blended, very smooth custard. Remove from fire; cool. Pour filling into prepared pastry; place lattice strips over top. Pinch edges lightly. Bake in moderately hot oven for 45 minutes or until mixture is firm but not dry and pastry is golden brown. Remove from oven; cool. Sprinkle with powdered sugar just before serving.

Serves 10.

ZABAGLIONE

MARSALA CUSTARD

6 egg yolks *6 level tsp. sugar*
6 half eggshells full of marsala (heavy sweet sherry)

Break egg yolks into top part of large double boiler. Add sugar. Beat with egg beater until light lemon color and thoroughly blended. Add marsala. Beat thoroughly again.

Place boiling water in lower part of double boiler. Cook egg-yolk mixture (over boiling water) about 5 minutes or until it begins to thicken. While cooking be sure to beat constantly. Do not allow to boil. Remove from fire immediately upon first sign of bubble. Cool. Place in refrigerator.

Serve cold in sherbet or parfait glasses. Serves 6.

TORTA DI RICOTTA

ITALIAN CHEESE PIE

Pastry:

2 cups flour *⅔ cup butter or shortening*
2 tbs. dry sherry *½ tsp. salt*

Sift together flour and salt. Cut in butter or shortening; gradually add sherry. If necessary, add a little water to hold mixture firmly. Do not knead too much. Roll in circular piece about ⅛ inch thick to fit 9- or 10-inch pie plate. Butter plate before placing pastry in it. Cut balance of pastry in strips ½ inch wide to use as crisscross (lattice) top.

Filling:

1½ lbs. ricotta (Italian cottage cheese)
¼ lb. toasted almonds
1 tbs. chopped citron
1 tsp. vanilla flavoring
4 eggs
⅓ cup granulated sugar
2 tbs. powdered sugar

Chop almonds fine; add ricotta and mix thoroughly. Beat eggs and granulated sugar well; add vanilla. Add to ricotta; stir until well blended and smooth.

Pour ricotta filling into prepared pastry; place lattice strips over top. Pinch edges lightly. Bake in moderately hot oven 45 minutes or until mixture is firm but not dry and pastry is golden brown. Remove from oven; cool. Sprinkle with powdered sugar just before serving.

Serves 10.

ZUPPA INGLESE #1

(Literally means "soup" but is an Italian rum cake covered with custard)

1 qt. milk
6 egg yolks
8 tbs. sugar
8 tbs. flour
1 grated lemon rind
12 tbs. sweet vermouth
12 tbs. sweet rum
6 tbs. orange marmalade
1 large spongecake (about 12 in.)
Pinch of salt
2 ozs. finely chopped toasted almonds

Plain Custard:

Beat egg yolks thoroughly. Blend well in saucepan the milk, eggs, sugar, flour, and salt. Strain through fine sieve to insure very smooth mixture. Grate lemon rind; add this to mixture. Cook over low flame for about 10 minutes or until thick and it *starts* to boil. Do not boil. Remove from fire. Cool. If chocolate flavor is desired, melt two cubes of bitter chocolate in hot custard. Stir well.

Spongecake:

8 egg yolks
8 egg whites
1⅓ cups flour
2 tsp. grated lemon rind
1¼ cup sugar
2 tbs. water
1½ tsp. almond extract
¼ tsp. salt

Use large mixing bowl. Sift ½ cup of sugar with flour several times to blend well. Place egg yolks, water, and grated lemon rind in mixing bowl. Beat lightly. Add almond extract. Gradually sift flour very lightly over beaten egg yolks. Fold in gently. Place egg whites in another bowl and beat until foamy. Add salt and balance of sugar; beat until stiff. Gently fold in the stiff egg whites into flour mixture. Pour into 10- or 12-inch ungreased cake pan. Bake in moderate oven 45 minutes, or until cake separates from sides of pan. Be careful not to jar cake while baking, as it may become heavy.

When cake is done, invert pan on wire rack for about 1 hour or until cold. Remove from pan.

Slice spongecake into 3 layers; pour 6 tablespoons of vermouth over each of 2 layers. Spread with thin layer of orange marmalade, then layer of custard. Place third layer over this; pour rum over all. Cover top and sides of cake evenly with thick layer of custard. Sprinkle with finely chopped almonds.

Serves 12 to 14.

ZUPPA INGLESE #2

ITALIAN RUM CAKE

8 egg yolks
8 half eggshells full of marsala (heavy sweet sherry)
8 level tsp. sugar
1 spongecake (10-12 in. in diameter)
1 cup sweet rum
2 tbs. sugar
½ pt. whipping cream
½ cup chopped glazed fruit

Zabaglione (Marsala Custard): Break egg yolks into

top part of large double boiler. Add sugar. Beat with egg beater until light lemon color and thoroughly blended. Add marsala; beat thoroughly again.

Place boiling water in lower part of double boiler. Cook egg-yolk mixture (over boiling water) about 5 minutes or until it begins to thicken. While cooking, be sure to beat constantly. Do not allow to boil. Remove from fire immediately upon first sign of bubble. Set aside to cool.

Slice spongecake into three layers. Place one layer on cake plate; pour ⅓ cup of rum over it. Cover with ⅓ of Zabaglione. Place second layer of cake over this; alternate with rum and Zabaglione. Place in refrigerator. When ready to serve, pour cream in mixing bowl; add 2 tablespoons of sugar; whip until stiff. Spread over top and sides of cake just before serving. Sprinkle with chopped glazed fruit.

Serves 12 to 14.

CHAPTER THIRTEEN

Luncheon Delicacies

Eggs

FRITTATA DI CARNE E VEGETALI

VEGETABLE-MEAT OMELET

6 eggs
1 sliced onion
6 tbs. olive oil
2 cups cooked meat and vegetables
4 tbs. grated Romano cheese
Salt and pepper to taste

Use any leftover meat and vegetables; chop fine. Heat 2 tablespoons of oil in large skillet. Brown onion about 3 minutes or until soft. Add meat and vegetables; mix well. Heat for 7 minutes; stir constantly. Transfer to mixing bowl. Beat eggs thoroughly in separate bowl; fold into omelet mixture; blend well.

Place balance of olive oil in frying pan. Heat. Fry omelet mixture about 5 minutes or until light brown on underside. Turn out carefully on a plate. If necessary, add more oil to frying pan. Slide omelet back into pan; brown other side.

Serve immediately. Serves 6 to 8.

FRITTATA DI BROCCOLI

BROCCOLI OMELET

1 small bunch broccoli
4 eggs
4 tbs. olive oil
1 clove garlic, chopped
3 tbs. grated Parmesan cheese
Salt and pepper to taste

Let broccoli stand in cold water 15 or 20 minutes. When crisp, peel; split stalks. Place in rapidly boiling salted water; cook about 15 minutes or until tender. Drain; cut crosswise in 1-inch pieces.

Beat eggs thoroughly in a large bowl; add salt, pepper, garlic, cheese, and broccoli; mix well.

Heat oil in large skillet; pour in mixture. Cook over low flame about 5 minutes or until omelet is fluffy and browned on under side. Turn carefully by using spatula. If necessary, place more oil in skillet. Brown on other side.

Serve immediately. Serves 4 to 6.

UOVA ALLA CACCIATORA

EGGS HUNTER'S STYLE

4 eggs
4 chicken livers
3 tbs. olive oil
4 tbs. warm water
¼ cup dry sauterne
1 tbs. tomato paste
1 tbs. chopped onion
Salt and pepper to taste

Cut livers in half; season with salt and pepper. Heat oil in frying pan; sauté livers and onion for 5 minutes over low flame.

Blend tomato paste and warm water in a cup. Add to livers; simmer for 5 minutes. Add sauterne; cook for 3 minutes. Add eggs one at a time, being careful not to break yolks. Cover pan and cook 3 minutes or until whites are firm.

Serve very hot on toast. Serves 4.

FRITTATA DI CIPOLLA

ONION OMELET

4 eggs
6 tbs. olive oil or butter
1 large sweet onion
Salt and pepper to taste

Break eggs into deep bowl; add salt and pepper to

taste; beat lightly. Slice onion wafer-thin. Heat half oil or butter in skillet. Brown onion slightly for about 5 minutes. Remove; place in bowl. Add eggs; beat well. Heat balance of oil in skillet; cook eggs over low flame 3 to 5 minutes or until omelet is light and fluffy and browned on under side. Using spatula, turn over carefully. Brown lightly.

Serve immediately. Serves 4.

UOVA FIORENTINA

EGGS FLORENTINE

4 eggs
3 tbs. olive oil
1½ lbs. fresh spinach
Salt and pepper to taste
4 tbs. grated Pecorino cheese

Clean, wash, and drain spinach carefully. Put oil in saucepan; when hot, add spinach. Cover well; cook 10 to 12 minutes or until tender. Add salt and pepper to taste.

Arrange spinach in four individual ramekins. Break an egg over each; sprinkle 1 tablespoon of grated Pecorino cheese over top. Bake in moderate oven about 3 minutes or until egg white is firm but yolk is still soft.

Serves 4.

UOVA CON OLIVE E PROVOLONE

EGGS WITH OLIVES AND PROVOLONE

4 eggs
3 tbs. olive oil
2 ozs. Provolone cheese
Salt and pepper to taste
12 large ripe Italian olives

Pit olives; cut in half. Beat eggs thoroughly. Cut cheese into ½-inch pieces. Heat oil in frying pan or skillet. Add olives; sauté for 2 minutes. Add cheese; stir constantly for 1 minute over medium flame. Fold in beaten eggs, pinch of pepper. (Use salt very sparingly since olives and cheese are salty.) Stir until eggs are as firm as desired.

Serve very hot. Serves 2.

UOVA CON PEPERONI

EGGS WITH PEPPERS

5 eggs
4 large firm green peppers
5 tbs. olive oil
1 clove garlic
Salt and pepper to taste

Clean, seed, and slice peppers lengthwise in 1-inch strips. Beat eggs thoroughly. Heat oil in large frying pan. When hot, add garlic and sliced peppers. Fry until slightly brown, about 5 minutes. Lower flame; cover pan; sauté slowly for 15 minutes or until peppers are soft. Fold in beaten eggs. Stir gently until eggs are of consistency desired. Remove from fire; serve immediately.

Serves 4.

UOVA CON SALSA DI POMODORO

EGGS WITH TOMATO SAUCE

6 eggs
4 tbs. olive oil
1 clove garlic, chopped
1 No. 2 can tomatoes
1 tbs. chopped parsley
Pinch of crushed red pepper seeds
1 small onion, sliced
Salt to taste

Heat olive oil in large shallow saucepan. Cook onion and garlic about 2 minutes or until soft. Add tomatoes, parsley, crushed pepper seeds, and salt to taste. Simmer over low flame about 25 minutes. Drop eggs in sauce one at a time, without breaking yolks. Cook slowly for 3 minutes or until egg whites are firm.

Serve hot. Serves 6.

ARANCINI DI RICOTTA

STUFFED RICE CROQUETTES

¾ lb. rice
1 lb. ricotta (Italian cottage cheese)
2 eggs, well beaten
1 cup toasted bread crumbs
½ cup olive or peanut oil
Salt to taste

Cook rice in 3 quarts of rapidly boiling salted water about 25 minutes or until done. Drain and cool, spread 1 tablespoon of rice on palm of hand; place 1 tablespoon of ricotta over rice; sprinkle with salt; top with more rice; shape into round or oblong croquettes. Continue until all rice and ricotta are used. Dip croquettes in well-beaten egg; roll in bread crumbs. Fry in very hot olive or peanut oil about 3 minutes or until golden brown on all sides.

Serve hot as side dish with meat or fowl. May be served also as a dessert. Simply roll in powdered sugar and serve hot or cold.

Serves 6 to 8.

CROCHE DI SPINACI

RICE-SPINACH CROQUETTES

1 cup cooked rice
3 cups cooked spinach
3 eggs, slightly beaten
½ tsp. salt
6 tbs. olive oil
2 ozs. grated Pecorino cheese
⅛ tsp. pepper

Mix all ingredients, except oil, thoroughly until well blended. Heat oil in skillet. Drop heaping tablespoons of mixture into hot oil; fry about 3 minutes or until each side is golden brown. Serve very hot as a side dish, or as a main dish with vegetables.

Serves 4.

CROCHE DI RISO

RICE CROQUETTES

½ lb. rice
2 eggs
4 ozs. grated Parmesan cheese
2 tbs. chopped parsley
1 cup toasted bread crumbs
2 cups peanut oil
Salt and pepper to taste

Wash and boil rice in 3 quarts of salted water for about 25 minutes or until soft. Drain and cool. Beat eggs lightly; add to rice. Add cheese and parsley; mix thoroughly. Roll into small balls (about size of walnut); dip in bread crumbs; fry in deep hot oil about 3 minutes or until golden brown. May be served as side dish with meat or fowl.

Serve hot. Serves 6.

RISOTTO MILANESE

RICE MILANESE

2 cups rice
1 large onion, sliced
4 ozs. grated Parmesan cheese
2 qts. chicken broth
½ lb. chopped chicken giblets
¼ lb. butter
½ tsp. saffron
Salt and pepper to taste

Cook giblets in pint of boiling salted water about 20 minutes or until tender. Remove; chop into small pieces.

Melt butter in large pot; fry onion over low flame about 5 minutes or until brown. Remove onion. Add cleaned, washed rice and stir for 5 minutes to prevent burning. Then add 1 cup of broth; stir constantly.

Dissolve saffron in ½ cup of broth; allow to stand 5 minutes. Then strain saffron; add colored broth to rice. Stir well. Gradually add remainder of broth as the rice absorbs it. When rice has cooked about ½ hour, add half the cheese and continue stirring.

Add giblets; stir constantly. Add additional cup of

broth if rice becomes too dry. Entire process takes about 45 minutes, and when done is moist and creamy. Add balance of grated Parmesan cheese.

Serves 6 to 8.

Other Luncheon Delicacies

CROCHE DI LATTE

MILK CROQUETTES

1 pt. lukewarm milk
2 ozs. butter
8 tbs. flour
1 cup bread crumbs
2 eggs
2 cups peanut oil
1 cup grated Romano cheese
1 tsp. chopped parsley
3 tbs. chopped cooked ham
Salt and pepper to taste

Dissolve butter in pan over low flame; add parsley. Cook about 3 minutes or until soft; stir constantly. Add flour slowly, stirring until it forms a soft ball. Add lukewarm milk slowly; stir constantly until mixture is a very smooth paste. This takes about 10 minutes. Remove from fire; add 1 egg, ham, and cheese; stir again.

Cool until firm by spreading out on large platter.

In the meantime, beat other egg thoroughly.

Take 1 heaping tablespoon of cooled mixture and roll into balls or croquettes. Dip in flour, then in beaten egg, and roll in bread crumbs. Fry in deep, very hot peanut oil about 2 minutes or until golden brown. May be served hot or cold. Serves 6.

FORMAGGIO CON OLIVE ALL'ARGENTIERA

CHEESE WITH OLIVES ARGENTIERA

½ lb. Italian black olives
¼ cup wine vinegar
¼ lb. Incanestrato cheese
3 tbs. olive oil

Cut cheese into 1-inch cubes. Heat oil in frying pan; add cheese and olives. Heat thoroughly over low flame about 15 minutes. Stir. Cheese grows slightly brown, does not melt. Add vinegar; boil up rapidly for 1 minute.

Serve very hot on toast. Serves 2 to 3.

FRITTELLE DI PATATE

POTATO PANCAKES

1½ lbs. potatoes
3 eggs
1 tbs. chopped parsley
1 cup peanut oil
1¼ cups bread crumbs
1 small onion, chopped
¼ cup grated Pecorino cheese
2 tbs. milk, if needed
Salt and pepper to taste

Boil and mash potatoes; cool. Place in deep mixing bowl. Beat eggs well; add to potatoes. Stir into mixture onion, cheese, parsley, ½ cup of bread crumbs, salt and pepper to taste. If too dry, add enough milk for easy molding.

Mold mixture into cakes about 2½ inches in diameter and ½ inch thick. Dip in balance of bread crumbs. Fry in hot oil about 5 minutes or until golden brown on both sides.

Serve very hot. Serves 4 to 6.

GUASTELLE CON FORMAGGIO

SICILIAN ROLLS WITH CHEESE

6 Sicilian rolls
½ lb. Provolone cheese
6 tsp. olive oil
½ lb. ricotta (Italian cottage cheese)
Salt and pepper to taste

Heat olive oil in small frying pan. Slice Provolone thin, about size of roll. Heat rolls in very hot oven 5 minutes to soften. Cut open through center.

Divide ricotta into 6 parts.

Pour 1 teaspoon of hot oil on one half of roll. Place slice of Provolone on it, then spread with portion of ricotta, a pinch of salt and pepper. Top with other half of roll and return to hot oven for 3 minutes. This forms a substantial sandwich.

Serve very hot. Serves 6.

GUASTELLE CON SALSICCIA

SICILIAN ROLLS WITH SAUSAGE

6 Sicilian rolls
6 links Italian sausage
3 large firm green peppers
6 tsp. olive oil
6 tbs. grated Romano cheese
Salt to taste

Broil sausage in very hot oven about 20 minutes or until golden brown and well done.

Cut peppers in half, take out seeds; broil in hot oven about 10 minutes or until light brown and tender. When cool, remove skins, if desired. Sprinkle with little salt.

Heat oil in frying pan. Heat rolls in very hot oven about 5 minutes to soften. Then cut open through center.

Place broiled sausage on roll; cover with broiled pepper; sprinkle lightly with grated cheese; pour 1 teaspoon of hot oil over all; cover with other half of roll. Return to oven for 3 minutes.

Serve very hot. Serves 6.

PATATE CON OLIVE

POTATOES WITH OLIVES

2 lbs. potatoes
3 tbs. butter
3 tbs. olive oil
¼ lb. black Italian olives
1 sliced onion
Salt and pepper to taste

Peel potatoes and slice thinly.

Melt butter in large frying pan; add oil; heat. Add sliced potatoes. Fry over high flame for 10 minutes; stir frequently to prevent sticking. Lower flame; add sliced onion; cook for about 20 minutes or until potatoes are done. Add salt and pepper, olives; stir; cook 5 minutes longer.

Serve hot. Serves 4 to 6.

POLENTA CON SALSICCIA

CORN MEAL WITH SAUSAGE

2 cups corn meal
6 cups water
1 tsp. salt
2 tbs. olive oil
1 clove garlic
1 lb. Italian sausage
2 tbs. chopped parsley
2 tbs. butter
1 No. 2 can plum tomatoes
2 ozs. grated Parmesan cheese
Salt and pepper to taste

Place water in top part of large double boiler and boil. As water bubbles rapidly, add salt. Gradually pour corn meal into water, stirring constantly to prevent lumping. Place boiling water in lower part of double boiler. Replace top of double boiler which contains corn-meal mixture. Cook slowly for 1 hour; stir frequently to insure creamy consistency.

Cut sausage into small serving pieces; fry in hot oil for 15 minutes. Add all ingredients except cheese; cover; cook over low flame about 1 hour.

To serve, spread half of hot corn meal on a very hot platter; cover with half of sauce. Place balance of corn meal on top; pour balance of sauce over this. Sprinkle generously with grated Parmesan cheese.

Serve very hot. Serves 6 to 8.

PIZZA SICILIANA

SICILIAN TOMATO PIE

1 lb. flour
1 tsp. salt
1 cup lukewarm water
8 anchovy filets
1 cake yeast
2 tbs. peanut or olive oil
2 cups Plain Tomato Sauce #2
½ cup grated Pecorino cheese

Dissolve yeast in lukewarm water. Place sifted flour and salt on board; add dissolved yeast. Knead thoroughly for

15 minutes. Add oil; continue kneading until smooth ball is obtained. Cover well. Set aside in warm place about 3 hours or until dough has raised to double its size.

In the meantime, prepare Plain Tomato Sauce #2. Cut anchovies into small pieces; add to sauce when done.

When dough has raised, spread in large well-greased baking pan about ½ to ¾inches thick. Dent here and there with finger tips. Pour generous layer of sauce over dough; sprinkle liberally with grated Pecorino cheese. Bake in hot oven for ½ hour. Lower heat; continue baking for 15 minutes or until *pizza* is golden brown.

Remove from oven; cut into pieces about 4 to 5 inches square. Serve very hot. Serves 4 to 6.

PIZZA CON SALSICCIA

PIZZA WITH SAUSAGE

Follow same recipe and quantities as for Pizza Siciliana. Add ½ pound of Italian sausage cut into small pieces; arrange on dough *before* putting on the sauce and cheese. Bake as for Pizza Siciliana.

PISELLI CON UOVA #1

PEAS WITH EGGS #1

2 lbs. fresh peas
6 hard-boiled eggs
2 sliced onions
¼ cup olive oil
1 cup hot water
Salt and pepper to taste

Shell peas. Heat half of oil in saucepan and cook onion about 5 minutes over slow flame or until soft. Add peas, ½ cup of water, salt, and pepper. Simmer; stir. As water is absorbed, gradually add more until peas are tender. This takes about 20 minutes.

Cut hard-boiled eggs in half lengthwise. Fry in balance of oil about 2 minutes or until slightly brown.

Place peas on hot serving dish and top with eggs.

Serve hot. Serves 4.

PISELLI CON UOVA #2

PEAS WITH EGGS #2

6 eggs
4 tbs. olive oil
1 large onion, chopped
1 No. 2 can tomatoes
1 can peas
Salt and pepper to taste

Heat oil in large shallow saucepan; add onion; cook about 2 minutes or until soft. Add tomatoes; simmer about 15 minutes. Add peas, salt, and pepper; simmer 10 minutes. Drop eggs in sauce one at a time. Be careful not to break yolks. Cook slowly about 3 minutes or until eggs are done.

Serves 6.

SUFFLE DI VERMICELLI E POMODORO

TOMATO-VERMICELLI SOUFFLÉ

1 cup canned tomatoes
3 tbs. olive oil
2 ozs. grated Parmesan cheese
½ lb. vermicelli
3 eggs
2 tbs. flour
Salt and pepper to taste

Heat oil over low flame in deep saucepan. Gradually stir in flour until well blended. Add tomatoes slowly; keep stirring. Bring to a boil; lower flame; simmer for 2 minutes. Add grated cheese, salt and pepper to taste; stir; turn off fire.

Break vermicelli into 1-inch pieces. Cook in 2 quarts of rapidly boiling salted water, about 6 minutes or until soft. Drain. Stir vermicelli into prepared sauce.

Beat egg yolks thoroughly; add. Beat egg whites stiff; fold in.

Transfer to buttered baking dish; bake in moderate oven about 10 minutes or until firm.

Serve hot. Serves 4.

Glossary of Italian Terms

Abbrustolito	Toasted
Acciughe	Anchovy filets
Acini di pepe	Pasta; pepper-kernel type
Affogati	Steamed
Agliata	With garlic
Aglio	Garlic
Agnellino	Baby lamb
Agro e dolce	Sour and sweet
Al; all'; alla	As; in the style of
Al burro	Buttered
Al dente	Medium-cooked
Al forno	Baked; roasted
All'aceto	In vinegar
Alla griglia	Broiled
All'olio	In oil
Amaretti	Macaroons
Aneto	Dill
Anguille	Eels
Anice	Anise seed
Anitra	Duck
Antipasto	Hors d'oeuvres
Aragosta	Lobster
Aranci	Oranges
Arancini	Croquettes
Aringhe	Herring
Arrostiti	Roasted
Asti Spumanti	Italian champagne
Autunno	Autumn
Baccalà	Dry cod
Bagaria	Sicilian village
Basilico	Basil leaf
Battesimo	Christening
Beccafico	Stuffed (Sicilian dialect)
Bel Paese	Brand name for mild cheese

Biscotti	Cookies; biscuits
Bistecca	Beefsteak
Bollito; bolliti	Boiled
Braciuolini	Rollettes
Broccoli	Broccoli
Brodo	Broth
Buon	Good
Buon Capo d'Anno	Happy New Year
Burro	Butter
Caciocavallo	Hard Sicilian cheese
Caffe espresso	Black coffee
Caffetiera	Coffee maker
Calamai	Squids (fish)
Cannella	Cinnamon
Capitone	Large eel
Capocollo	Smoked pork
Capo d'Anno	New Year
Cappelletti	"Little Hats"; moist pasta
Capperi	Capers
Carciofi	Artichokes
Carciofini	Artichoke hearts
Carne	Meat
Carnevale	Carnival
Cassata	Cream tart
Cassatelle	Cream tartlets
Cavatoni rigati	Pasta; ribbed curved type
Cavolfiore	Cauliflower
Cavolo	Cabbage
Cervelli	Brains
Cervo	Venison
Chianti	Dry table wine; white or red
Chiodo di garofini	Cloves
Cicoria	Dandelion
Cipolla	Onion
Colla; coll'	With
Compleanno	Birthday
Con	With; and
Con carne	With meat
Conchiglie	Pasta; sea-shell type
Coniglio	Rabbit

Costatelle	Chops
Costatelle di vitella	Veal chops
Cotolette	Cutlets
Cresima	Confirmation
Croche	Croquettes
Cucuzza	Light green Italian squash
Di; d'	Of
Ditali	Pasta; short tubular type
Ditalini	Pasta; very short tubular type
Dolce	Sweet; sweetened; sweets
Dolci	Sweet; sweets
E	And
Escarola	Escarole
Estate	Summer
Fagiano	Pheasant
Fagioli	Beans
Fagiolini	String beans
Farfallette	Pasta; butterfly or bowknot type
Fava	Fresh green bean; also dried
Fegatini	Chicken livers
Fegato	Liver
Festa	Holiday
Festa di San Giuseppe	St. Joseph's Day
Feste	Holidays
Feste invernale	Winter holidays
Fetucci	Pasta; bowknot type
Filetti	Filets
Filetto	Filet mignon
Fina	Fine; small
Finocchio	Anise-flavored Italian celery
Fiorentina	Florentine style
Foglie di alloro	Bay leaves
Formaggio	Cheese
Forno	Oven
Frittata	Omelet

Frittelle	Pancakes
Fritto; fritti	Fried
Funghi	Mushrooms
Fusilli	Pasta; curly spaghetti type
Gamberi	Shrimps
Giuseppe	Joseph
Gnocchi	Dumplings
Gorgonzola	Cheese; Roquefort type
Griglia	Broiled; a grill
Guastelle	Sicilian rolls
Imbottiti; imbottite	Stuffed
Incanestrato	Sicilian grating cheese
Inglese	English
Insalata	Salad
Inverno	Winter
Lasagne	Wide noodles
Latte	Milk
Lattuga Romana	Romaine (lettuce)
Lesso	Boiled
Linguini	Narrow noodles
Lumache	Snails
Mafalde	Pasta; twisted noodles
Maggiorana	Marjoram
Maiale	Pork
Mandorla	Almond
Manteca	Cheese and butter combined
Manzo	Beef
Marinara	Mariner style
Marineo	Sicilian village near Palermo
Marsala	Heavy sweet sherry
Melenzana	Eggplant
Menta	Mint
Merluzzo	Whiting
Mezzani	Pasta; curved type
Milanese	Milan style
Minestra	Thick vegetable soup

Minestrone	Thick soup
Mostaccioli	Pasta; oblique hollow type
Mozzarella	Moist unsalted cheese
Mozzarella affumicata	Smoked Mozzarella
Natale	Christmas
Noce Moscata	Nutmeg
Nonni	Grandmother
Notte di Capo d'Anno	New Year's Eve
Olio	Oil
Olio d'oliva	Olive oil
Olive	Olives
Olive nere	Black olives
Olive nere all'olio	Black olives in oil
Oregano	Herb; orégano; more delicate than thyme
Oreganato	With orégano
Ossi buchi	Veal shanks
Ostriche	Oysters
Palermitana	Palermo style
Pane	Bread
Pane abbrustolito	Toast
Parmigiano	Parmesan cheese
Pasta	Paste; dough; macaroni
Pasticcio	Pastry; piecrust
Pastina	Pasta; tiny disk type
Pastina al uovo	Pasta; made with egg
Patate	Potatoes
Pecorino	Goat's-milk cheese
Pepe forte	Crushed red pepper seeds
Peperoni	Green peppers
Peperoncini	Small peppers
Peperoncini all'aceto	Small green peppers in vinegar
Perciatelli	Pasta; long hollow type
Pere	Pears
Pernice	Partridge
Pesca	Peach
Pesce	Fish
Pesche	Peaches

Pesciolini	Minnows; tiny fish
Piazza	Public square
Piccante	Piquant
Piccione	Pigeon
Pignoli	Pine nuts
Pimiento	Sweet red pepper
Piselli	Peas
Pizza	Pie
Pizzaiola	"Like a little pie"
Polenta	Yellow corn meal
Pollo	Chicken; fowl
Polpette	Meat balls
Polpettini	Small meat balls
Polpettone	Meat loaf
Pomodoro	Tomato
Prezzemolo	Parsley
Primavera	Springtime
Prosciutto	Italian ham
Provolone	Mild slicing cheese
Quaglia	Quail
Radici	Radishes
Ravioli	Moist stuffed pasta
Ricotta	Italian cottage cheese
Ricotta salata	Very dry ricotta
Rigatoni	Pasta; large ribbed type
Ripieno	Stuffed; filled; stuffing
Riso	Rice
Rognoni	Kidneys
Rollini	Rollettes
Romano	Romano style
Romano	Tangy grating cheese
Rosamarina	Herb; rosemary
Rosso	Red
Salami	Smoked Italian sausage
Salmone	Salmon
Salsa	Sauce
Salsa semplice	Plain sauce
Salsiccia	Sausage
Salsiccia con peperoni	Sausage with peppers; hot sausage

Salsiccia secca	Very dry pork sausage
Salute!	Greetings! (a toast)
Salvia	Herb; sage
San Giuseppe	St. Joseph
Sarde	Sardines
Savoiardi	Lady fingers
Scaloppine	Thin veal cutlets
Scamozza	Pear-shaped cheese
Scappati	Fleeting; like a bird
Sciacca	Sicilian fishing village
Sedani	Celery hearts
Selvaggio	Wild
Semplice	Plain; simple
Sfinge	Cream puffs
Sgombro	Mackerel
Siciliana	Sicilian style
Sogliole	Sole
Spada	Swordfish
Spaghetti	Pasta; thin type
Spaghettini	Pasta; very thin type
Sparagi	Asparagus
Spiedini	Skewered; meat rolls on skewers
Spinaci	Spinach
Spinola	Striped bass
Sposalizio	Wedding
Spumoni	Italian ice cream
Stocco	Stockfish
Strachino	Tangy goat's-milk cheese
Strufoli	Clusters
Suffle	Soufflé
Tagliarini	Pasta; very narrow egg noodles
Tartufata	Truffle
Timo	Thyme
Tonno	Tuna fish
Torta	Tart; pie
Trippa	Tripe
Trota	Trout
Tubettini	Pasta; tiny tubular type

Uccelli scappati	Veal birds (northern Italian dialect)
Umido	Stew
Uova	Eggs
Uovo	Egg
Uovo di aringhe	Herring roe
Uovo di tonno	Tuna-fish roe
Vermicelli	Pasta; very thin type
Vigilia di Natale	Christmas Eve
Vitella	Veal
Vongoli	Clams
Zafferano	Herb; saffron
Zia	Aunt
Zio	Uncle
Ziti	Pasta; tubular type
Zucchini	Italian squash
Zuppa	Soup

Standard Measurements

2 cups butter or shortening	1 lb.
4 cups flour	1 lb.
2 cups sugar (granulated)	1 lb.
2 cups rice	1 lb.
2 cups	1 pt.
4 cups	1 qt.
4 qts.	1 gal.
4 tbs. flour	1 oz.
2 level tbs. butter or shortening	1 oz.
4 tbs.	¼ cup
16 tbs.	1 cup
3 tsp. liquid	1 tbs.
2 tbs. liquid	1 oz.
16 ozs. solids	1 lb.
16 ozs. liquid	1 pt.
25 drops of thin liquid	1 tsp.

All measurements are level

Index

Index

Acciughe, 29, 151
Acini di Pepe, 9, 151
Aglio, 5, 151
Agnellino al Forno, 77
Agnello
  con Riso, 78-79
  in Umido con Cucuzza, 79
Amaretti, 19, 123-24, 151

ANCHOVY. *See also* Appetizers
  and Broccoli, 93
  Sauce, 53
  with Artichokes, 96
  with Escarole, 97-98
  with *Fusilli,* 41-42
  with Mariner Sauce, 49
  with Peppers, 102
  with *Pizza,* 148-49
  with Spaghetti, 46-47
  with Trout, 68
Aneto, 5, 151
Anguille Marinate, 60
Anice, 5, 151
Aniseed. *See Anice*
Anise Slices, 22, 26, 124
Anitra al Cognac, 114
Antipasto, 28-30. *See also* Appetizers

APPETIZERS, 28-30
  Acciughe, 29, 151
  Anchovy Filets, 29
  Anise-Flavored Celery, 29-30
  Artichoke Hearts, 29
  Capocollo, 29, 152
  Carciofini, 29, 152
  Celery Hearts, 30
  Finocchio, 29-30, 153
  Funghi con Aceto e Olio, 30
  Green Peppers, 30
  Ham, 30
  Herring Roe, 30
  Menus, 29
  Mushrooms, 30
  Olive Nere all'Olio, 30, 155
  Olives, 30
  Peperoncini all'Aceto, 29, 30, 155
  Pimiento, 30
  Pork, 29
  Prosciutto, 30, 156
  Radishes, 30
  Salami, 30, 156
  Salsiccia Secca, 30, 157
  Sausage, 30
  Sedani, 30, 157
  Tuna Fish Roe, 30
  Uovo di Aringhe, 30, 158
  Uovo di Tonno, 30, 158
Aragosta
  alla Marsala, 69
  fra Diavolo, 68-69
  Marinara, 70
  Oreganata, 69-70
Arancini di Ricotta, 143

ARTICHOKES, 94-96
  Boiled, 95

Fried, 95-96
Roasted, 94-95
Stuffed, 96

ASPARAGUS
Parmesan, 103
with Noodles, 52
with *Tagliarini*, 52
Asti Spumanti, 15, 25, 151
Baccalà
Dolce e Agro, 58
Fiorentina, 58-59

BACON
with Beef, 74
with Lamb, 77
with Partridge, 115
with Pigeon, 115, 116
with Quail, 121
with Rabbit, 111
with Veal Birds, 86
with Venison, 110

BASIL, 6
in Kidneys, 90
in Lobster, 69
in Minnow Pancakes, 61
in Mushroom Sauce, 55
in Salad, 105
in Shrimp, 71
in *Spaghettini*, 51
in Tomato Sauce, 56
in Tuna, 66
in Veal, 82-83
Bass, 65
Beans. *See* Kidney Beans, String Beans, Vegetables

BEEF
à la Mode, 76
Braciuolini di Manzo, 74-75
Bistecca Milanese, 74
Brodo di Manzo, 34
Broth, 34
Filet Mignon, 75
Filetto, 75
Manzo alla Moda, 76
Meat Balls, 75
Milanese, 74
Rollettes, 74
Skewered Chopped, 76-77
Spiedini alla Romana, 76-77
Steak, 74
Stew, 92
Birthday Menu, 20. *See also* Menus
Biscotti
al'Anici, 124
di Zia Lena, 124-25
Bistecca Milanese, 74
Bow Knots, Sweet, 127
Braciuolini
d'Agnello, 78
di Manzo, 74-75
Brains, 86-87

BROCCOLI
alla Siciliana, 93
con Olive, 93
Omelet, 139-40
Sicilian, 93
with Olives, 93
Brodo
di Manzo, 34
di Pesce con Tagliarini, 33

BROTH. *See also* Soups
Beef, 34
Fish, 33

BURGUNDY WINE, 13, 20, 21, 23, 24
with Beef, 76
with Kidneys, 90
with Peaches, 129
with Piquant Sauce, 55
with Pork, 80

with Rabbit, 112
with Sausage, 91

CABBAGE
Stuffed, 96-97
with Pork Chops, 80

CACCIATORA-STYLE
Chicken, 117-18
Eggs, 140
Rabbit, 112
Veal Chops, 81-82
Caciocavallo Cheese, 7, 17, 152
with Stuffed Artichokes, 96

CAFFE ESPRESSO, 122, 152
Caffettiera for, 122, 123, 152

CAKES. *See also* Desserts
Cassata, 125
Cheese, 135
Cream Tart, 125
De Luxe Cream, 127
Pine-Nut Clusters, 130-31
Rum, 136, 137
Sponge, 136, 137
Torta di Ricotta, 135
Calamai con Pomodoro, 59

CAPERS, 6
in Eggplant, 94
Sauce, 53
with Spaghetti, 51
with Stockfish, 66
Capitone, 18, 22, 152
Fritto, 59-60
Capocollo, 29, 152
Caponata alla Siciliana, 94
Cappelletti, 9, 19, 22, 27, 40, 152
Carciofi
Arrostiti, 94-95, 152
Bolliti, 95
Fritti, 95-96
Imbottiti alla Siciliana, 96
Carnival Menu, 21. *See also* Menus

CARROTS
with Beef, 76
with Chicken Soup, 35
with *Minestrone*, 34, 37
with Rabbit, 111
with Spinach Soup, 36
with Vegetable Soup, 35
with Venison, 110
Cassata alla Siciliana, 19, 22, 125, 152
Cassatelle alla Siciliana, 126, 152
Cauliflower with Fusilli, 41
Cavolo Imbottito, 96
Celery and *Minestra*, 39
Cervelli Impanati, 86-87
Cervo alla Mario, 110
Cheese
pie, 135
with Olives, 145-46

CHEESES, 7-8. *See also* names of cheeses
Bel Paese, 7, 151
Caciocavallo, 7, 152
Gorgonzola, 7, 154
Incanestrato, 7, 154
Manteca, 8, 154
Mozzarella, 8, 155
Mozzarella-Affumicata, 8, 155
Parmigiano, 8, 155
Pecorino, 8, 155
Provolone, 8, 156
Ricotta, 8, 156
Ricotta Salata, 8, 156
Romano, 8, 156
Scamozza, 8, 157
Strachino, 8, 157

CHICKEN, 116-21
Buttered, 116
Cacciatora, 117
Livers, 51
Marsala, 118
Orégano, 120-21
Soup, 35
Stew, 120
Stuffed, 119
with Mushrooms, 118
with Rosemary, 119
Chops. *See* Pork, Veal
Christening Menu, 21. *See also* Menus
Christmas Menu, 23. *See also* Menus
Cicoria Fina Agliata, 97

CLAMS
on Toast, 72-73
Sauce, 57
Steamed, 73
with Spaghetti, 50
Claret Wine, 13, 20, 22, 24, 25
with Liver, 87-88

CODFISH
Florentine, 58-59
Sweet and Sour, 58

COFFEE, 122
Cognac with Duck, 114
Conchiglie e Patate, 41
Confirmation Menu, 22. *See also* Menus
Coniglio
al Forno, 111
alla Cacciatora, 112
Dolce e Agro, 113
Fritto, 111

COOKIES
Amaretti, 123
Anise Slices, 124
Aunt Lena's, 124
Lady Fingers, 132
Macaroons, 123
Corn Meal with Sausage, 148
Costatelle
di Maiale, 80
di Maiale con Cavolo, 80
di Vitella Cacciatora, 81-82
Cotolette
alla Parmigiana, 82
di Vitella, 82, 153
Cream Puffs, St. Joseph's, 131-32
Cream Tart Sicilian, 125
Cream Tartlets Sicilian, 126
Croche
di Latte, 145
di Riso, 144
di Spinaci, 143

CROQUETTES, 143-44
Milk, 145
Rice, 143-45
Custard, Marsala, 135
Customs, 12-28. *See also* Festivals, Menus
Cutlets. *See* Veal

DANDELIONS
Salad, 105, 106
Sautéed, 97
De Luxe Cream Cake, 20, 127

DESSERTS
Amaretti, 123-24
Anise Slices, 124
Bow Knots, 127
Caffe Espresso, 122, 152
Cassata, 125, 152
Cassatelle, 126, 152
Cheese Pie Italian, 135
Coffee, 122

Cookies, 124
Cream Cake, 127
Cream Puffs, 131-32
Cream Tart, 125
Cream Tartlets, 126
Custard, 136
De Luxe Cream Cake, 127
Ice Cream, 133
Lady Fingers, 131
Macaroons, 123-24
Marsala Custard, 135
Orange Balls, 128
Pallottole d'Aranci, 128
Peaches with Almonds, 130
Peaches with Burgundy, 129
Pears, 129
Pie Crust, 130
Pignolata-Strufoli, 130-31
Pine-Nut Clusters, 130-31
Pistachio Pie, 134
Rum Cake, 136, 137
Sponge Cake, 128-29
Spumoni, 133, 157
St. Joseph's *Sfinge,* 131
Torta di Ricotta, 135
Zabaglione, 135
Zuppa Inglese, 136, 137
Ditalini in *Minestrone,* 38
Ditali Pie, 52
Duck, Brandied, 114

Easter Menu, 25. *See also* Menus

EELS, 18, 22, 152
Fried, 59-60
Marinated, 60

EGGPLANT, 94, 100-101
Broiled, 101
Diced, 94
Fried, 100
Parmesan, 100
with Spaghetti, 49
EGGS, 139-42. *See also* Luncheon Delicacies, Salads
Broccoli Omelet, 130-40
Cacciatora, 140
Florentine, 141
Hunter's Style, 140
Onion Omelet, 140-41
Vegetable-Meat Omelet, 139
with Olives and *Provolone,* 141
with Peas, 149-50
with Peppers, 142
with Tomato Sauce, 142
Escarola
Imbottita, 97
Sauté, 98

ESCAROLE
Salad, 105, 107
Sautéed, 98
Stuffed, 97

Fagiano o Coniglio Selvaggio, 114-15
Fagiolini Sauté, 98
Farfallette Dolci, 127, 153
Fegato
con Funghi alla Griglia, 87
con Vino, 87-88

FENNEL. *See also Finocchio* Salad, 106
with Spaghetti, 47
Festival Menus. *See* Menus

FESTIVALS, 14-27. *See also* Menus
Carnival, 17
Christmas, 18-19
Easter, 17-18

New Year's, 14-15
New Year's Eve, 15
St. Joseph's Day, 16-17
Filet Mignon, 75
Filet of Sole Pizzaiola, 64
Filetti di Sogliole Pizzaiola, 64
Filetto Siciliana, 75
Finocchio, 29, 153
Salad, 106
Spaghetti with, 47-48

FISH, 81-93. *See also* names of fish, Shellfish
Bass, 65
Broth, 33
Cod, 58-59
Eels, 59-60
Filet of Sole, 64
Mackerel, 63
Minnow Pancakes, 61
Salmon, 62
Sardines, 62-63
Soup, 33
Squids, 59
Stockfish, 65-66
Striped Bass, 65
Swordfish, 64
Trout, 68
Tuna, 66-67
Whiting, 60-61
Formaggio con Olive all'Argentiera, 145-46
Fowl, 114-21. *See also* Chicken, Duck, Partridge, Pheasant, Pigeon, Quail
Frittata
di Broccoli, 139-40
di Carne e Vegetali, 139
di Cipolla, 140
Frittelle
di Patate, 146
di Pesciolini, 61

FRUIT. *See also* names of fruits
Lemon and Orange Salad, 104
Orange Balls, 128
Peaches with Almonds, 130
Peaches with Burgundy, 129
Stuffed Pears, 129
Funghi
alla Parmigiana, 99
con Aceto, 30
Imbottiti, 99
Fusilli, 9, 154
with Cauliflower, 41
Gamberi
alla Mario, 70-71
con Riso, 71

GAME, 110-14
Rabbit, 111-114
Venison, 110

GLOSSARY OF ITALIAN TERMS, 151-58
Gnocchi, 42, 154

GORGONZOLA CHEESE, 7, 154
Salad Dressing, 109
Guastelle
con Formaggio, 146
con Salsiccia, 147

HAM, ITALIAN
Prosciutto, 29, 30, 156
with Beef, 77
with Chicken, 119
with Veal, 83, 84

HERBS, 5-7. *See also names of herbs*
Aglio, 5, 151
Aneto, 5, 151
Anice, 5, 151

Aniseed, 5
Basil, 6
Basilico, 6, 151
Bay Leaves, 6
Cannella, 6, 152
Capers, 6
Capperi, 6, 152
Chiodi di Garofoni, 6, 152
Cinnamon, 6
Cipolla, 6, 152
Cloves, 6
Dill, 5
Foglie di Alloro, 6, 153
Garlic, 5
Maggiorana, 6, 154
Marjoram, 6
Menta, 6, 154
Mint, 6
Noce Moscata, 6, 155
Nutmeg, 6
Onion, 6
Oregano, 6, 155
Parsley, 6
Pepe Forte, 6, 155
Prezzemolo, 6, 156
Red Pepper Seeds, 6, 155
Rosamarina, 7, 156
Rosemary, 7
Saffron, 7
Sage, 7
Salvia, 7, 157
Thyme, 7
Timo, 7, 157
Zafferano, 7, 158
Hunter's Style. *See Cacciatora*

Ice Cream, 133. *See also Spumoni*
Incanestrato Cheese, 7, 154
with Noodles, 51
with Olives, 145
Insalata
d'Arancio e Limone, 104
d'Escarola, 105
di Calamai, 105
di Cicoria Fina, 105
di Fagiolini, 106
di Finocchio, Pomodoro e Cicoria, 106
di Lattuga Romana, 107
di Patate e Uova, 107-108
di Pomodoro con Oregano, 108
Mista, 107
Italian Ham. *See* Ham, Italian
Italian Ice Cream. *See Spumoni*

KIDNEY BEANS
Minestra, 39, 154
Soup, 38
Kidneys with Burgundy, 90

La Crema, 20, 127
Lady Fingers, 132

LAMB, 77-79
Agnellino al Forno, 77
Agnello con Riso, 78-79
Agnello in Umido, 79
Braciuolini, 78, 152
Roast, 25, 27, 77-78
Rollettes, 78
Stew, 79, 92
with Rice, 78-79
Lasagne, 9, 23, 42-43, 154. *See also* Noodles, Spaghetti, *Pasta*
al Forno, 43
Imbottite, 42
Lemon and Orange Salad, 21, 104
Lentil Soup, 37
"Little Hats," 19, 40

LIVER
with Claret, 87-88

with Mushrooms, 87

LOBSTER, 68-70
Fra Diavalo, 68
Mariner, 70
Marsala, 69
Orégano, 69
Lumache Siciliana, 71-72

LUNCHEON DELICACIES, 139-50. *See also* Cheese Croquettes, Eggs, names of cheeses, Rice
Corn Meal with Sausage, 148
Peas with Eggs, 149-50
Pizza, 148, 149, 156
Polenta, 148, 156
Potato Pancakes, 146
Potatoes with Olives, 147
Rolls with Cheese, 146
Rolls with Sausage, 147
Tomato-*Vermicelli* Soufflé, 150

MACARONI, 44-45
Muffs, 44
with *Ricotta,* 45
Macaroons, 123-24
Mackerel, 63
Maialino Arrostito, 15, 21, 24
Manicotti, 44
Manzo alla Moda, 76
Marinara. See Mariner Sauce
Mariner Sauce, 49
with Lobster, 70
with Spaghetti, 49

MARSALA WINE, 14, 23, 24, 25, 26, 27
Custard, 135
with Chicken, 118
with Filet Mignon, 75
with Lobster, 69
with *Scaloppine,* 84
with *Zabaglione,* 135
with *Zuppa Inglese,* 137

MEASUREMENTS, 158
Meat Sauce, 54
with Spaghetti, 48

MEATS, 74-92. *See also* Beef, Lamb, Pork, Sauces, Soups, Stews, Veal
Brains, 86-87
Cervelli Impanati, 86-87
Fegato con Funghi, 87, 153
Fegato con Vino, 87-88
Kidneys with Burgundy, 90
Liver, 87-88
Meat Loaf, 88-89
Polpettone, 88-89, 156
Rognoni, 90, 156
Salsiccia alla Griglia, 90
Salsiccia con Vino, 91
Sausage, 90-91
Stew, 92
Tripe, 91
Trippa Milanese, 91
Umido di Carne, 92
Melenzana
alla Griglia, 101
alla Parmigiana, 100
Fritta, 100

MENUS, 20-27, 29. *See also* Festivals
Appetizer, 29
Autumn, 26
Birthday, 20
Carnival, 21
Christening, 21
Christmas, 23
Christmas Eve, 22
Confirmation, 22
Easter, 25
New Year's, 24

New Year's Eve, 23
Spring, 25
St. Joseph's Day, 24
Summer, 26
Wedding, 27
Winter, 26
Winter Holiday, 27
Merluzzo
con Salsa di Pomodoro, 61
Lesso, 60

MILANESE STYLE
Beefsteak, 74
Minestrone, 34
Ossi Buchi, 83, 155
Pears, 129
Rice, 144
Tripe, 91
Milk Croquettes, 145
Minestra
Aunt Tessie's, 39
di Pasta e Fagioli, 38
di Zia Teresa, 39
Minestrone, 155. *See also* Soups
di Zio Giuseppe, 37
Milanese, 34
Plain, 38
Semplice, 38
Uncle Joe's, 37

MINT
in Cod, 58
in Liver, 87
in Mackerel, 63
in Salads, 105
in Swordfish, 64
in Trout, 68
in Tuna, 67
Mixed Salad, 107

MOZZARELLA CHEESE, 8, 155
with Chopped Beef, 77
with Eggplant, 100
with Meat Loaf, 88
with Noodles, 43
with Stuffed Noodles, 42

MUSHROOMS
Antipasto, 30
Parmesan, 99
Stuffed, 99
with Chicken, 118
with Liver, 87
with Mackerel, 63
with Meat Sauce, 54
with *Rigatoni,* 46
with Tomato Sauce, 55

New Year's Eve Menu, 23
See also Menus
New Year's Menu, 24. *See also* Menus
Nonni's kitchen, 1-11

NOODLES, 42-43. *See also Lasagne*
Baked, 43
Stuffed, 42
with Asparagus, 52
with Livers, 51

Olive Nere all'Olio, 30, 155
Olive Oil, 3-5

OLIVES
with Broccoli, 93
with Eggs and *Provolone,* 141
with *Incanestrato* Cheese, 145
with Potatoes, 147
with Stockfish, 65-66
Omelets. *See* Eggs
Onion Omelet, 140-41

ORANGE
Balls, 128
Salad, 104

OREGANO, 6, 155
in Chicken, 120-21
in Clams, 73
in Filet of Sole, 64
in Lamb, 79
in Lobster, 69
in Mariner Sauce, 49
in Mushrooms, 99
in Oysters, 72
in Salad, 108
in Squids, 59
in Stockfish, 65
in Swordfish, 64
in Tomato Sauce, 56
Ossi Buchi alla Milanese, 83, 155
Ostriche alla Mario, 72
Oysters Mario, 72

Pallottole d'Aranci, 19, 128

PANCAKES
Minnow, 61
Potato, 146
Pane di Spagna, 128

PARMESAN CHEESE, 8
with Asparagus, 103
with Brains, 86-87
with Broccoli Omelet, 139-40
with Corn Meal and Sausage, 148
with Eggplant, 100
with Fish Broth, 33
with "Little Hats," 40
with Lobster, 69
with Macaroni, 45
with Meat Loaf-Potato Filling, 88
with *Minestrone,* 38
with Mushrooms, 99
with Noodles, 43, 52
with *Ravioli,* 45
with Rice, 144
with Soufflé, 150
with Spaghetti, 47, 49
with Spinach Soup, 36
with Stuffed Noodles, 42
with Tripe, 91
with Veal, 82
Parmigiano Cheese, 8, 155. *See also* Parmesan Cheese
Partridge, Roasted, 115

PASTA, 8-11. *See also* Macaroni, Noodles, Spaghetti
Acini di Pepe, 9, 151
Baked Noodles, 43
Cappelletti, 9, 40, 152
Cavatoni Rigati, 9, 152
Conchiglie, 9, 41, 152
con Ricotta, 45
Ditali, 9, 52, 153
Ditalini, 9, 38, 153
Dumplings, 42
Egg Noodles, 52
Farfallette, 9, 153
Fusilli, 9, 41, 154
Gnocchi, 42, 154
Lasagne, 9, 42-43, 154
Linguini, 10, 154
"Little Hats," 40
Macaroni, 44, 45
Mafalde, 10, 154
Mezzani, 10, 154
Mostaccioli, 10, 155
Noodles, 42-43, 51-52
Pastina, 10, 155
Pastina al Uovo, 10, 155
Perciatelli, 10, 155
Ravioli, 10, 45, 156
Rigatoni, 10, 46, 156
Sea Shells, 41
Spaghetti, 10, 46-52, 157
Spaghettini, 10, 51, 157
Tagliarini, 11, 51, 52, 157

Tubettini, 11, 38, 157
Vermicelli, 11, 37, 158
Ziti, 11, 158
Pasticcio, 130, 155
Patate con Olive, 147

PEACHES
with Almonds, 130
with Burgundy, 129

PEAS
Sauce, 55
with Eggs, 149-50
with Shrimp, 71

PECORINO CHEESE, 8, 155
with Eggplant, 101
with Eggs Florentine, 141
with Pancakes, 146
with *Pizza* and Sausage, 149
with Rice Spinach Croquettes, 143
with *Rigatoni,* 46
with Sea Shells, 41
with Spaghetti, 48, 51
with Tomato *Pizza,* 148
with Veal, 82
Peperoncini all'Aceto, 29, 30, 155
Peperoni, 101-102, 155
Arrostiti, 101
Fritti, 102
Imbottiti, 102

PEPPERS, 101-102
Fried, 102
Roasted, 101
Stuffed, 102
with Anchovy, 102
with Eggs, 142
with *Romano,* 102
with Veal, 85
Pere Ripiene alla Milanese, 129
Pernice al Forno, 115
Pesca con Vino Rosso, 130
Pesche Imbottite alla Mandorla, 130
Pheasant Mario, 27, 114
Piccione Sauté, 115
Piccioni Ripieni, 116

PIE
Cheese, 135-36
Crust, 130
Pistachio, 134
Pizza, 148-49
Tomato, 148

PIGEONS, 115-16
Sautéed, 115
Stuffed, 116
Pignolata-Strufoli, 19, 23, 130
Pine-Nut Clusters, 19, 130
Piquant Sauce, 55
Piselli con Uova, 149-50
Pistachio Pie, 21, 134
Pizza, 156
con Salsiccia, 149
Siciliana, 148
Sicilian Tomato Pie, 148
with Sausage, 149
Polenta
con Salsiccia, 148
with Sausage, 148
Pollo
al Burro, 116
alla Cacciatora, 117
colla Marsala, 118
con Funghi, 118
con Rosamarina, 119
Imbottito, 119
in Umido, 120
Polpette, 75, 156
Polpettone, 88-89, 156
con Patate, 88
con Ricotta, 89

PORK, 80-81
Chops, 80

Costatelle con Cavolo, 80
Costatelle di Maiale, 80
Maialino Arrostito, 81
Roasted Suckling Pig, 81

POTATOES
and Egg Salad, 107
Dumplings, 42
Gnocchi, 42, 154
Meat Loaf, 88
Meat Stew, 92
Minestra, 38-39
Minestrone, 37-38
Pancakes, 146
with Olives, 147
with Rabbit Stew, 113
with Sea Shells, 41
Prosciutto, 29, 30, 156

PROVOLONE CHEESE, 8, 156
with Eggs and Olives, 141
with Rolls, 146

Quaglia alla Griglia, 121
Quail, Broiled, 121

RABBIT
Cacciatora, 112
Fried, 111
Roasted, 111
Stew, 113
Sweet and Sour, 113
Wild, 114-15
Ravioli, 10, 45, 156

RICE, 143-45. *See also* Croquettes
and Spinach Soup, 36
Croquettes, 143-44
Milanese, 144
with Lamb, 78-79
with Peppers, 102
with Shrimp, 71
with Veal, 85

RICOTTA CHEESE, 8, 156
with Cheese Pie, 136
with Cream Tart, 125
with Croquettes, 143
with "Little Hats," 40
with Macaroni, 45
with Meat Loaf, 89
with Rolls, 146
with St. Joseph's Cream Puffs, 131
with Stuffed Noodles, 42
with Tartlet, 126
Rigatoni con Salsiccia, 46
Risotto Milanese, 20
Rognoni al Vino Rosso, 90

ROLLETTES
Beef, 74
Lamb, 78
Spiedini, 76
Veal, 83-84
Rollini di Vitella, 83-84

ROLLS
with Cheese, 146
with Sausage, 147
Romaine Salad, 107

ROMANO CHEESE, 8, 156
with Beef, 76
with Cabbage, 96
with Chicken, 119
with Croquettes, 145
with *Ditali* Pie, 52
with Macaroni Muffs, 44
with Mackerel, 63
with Meat Balls, 75
with Meat Loaf, 88, 89
with Milk Croquettes, 145
with *Minestra,* 39

with *Minestrone,* 37
with Pancakes, 61
with Peppers, 102
with Pigeon, 116
with Rolls and Sausage, 147
with Sardines, 62
with Soup, 38
with Spaghetti, 49, 50
with Veal, 84, 85
with *Zucchini,* 104
Roquefort Cheese Dressing, 109

ROSEMARY
in Chicken, 119
in Eels, 60
in Lamb, 78
in Piquant Sauce, 55
in Rabbit, 112
in Veal, 86
Rum Cake, 136, 137. *See also* Cakes

SALAD DRESSINGS, 108-109
Gorgonzola, 109
Italian, 109
Roquefort, 109
Sweet Basil, 108

SALADS, 104-108
Dandelion, 105
Escarole, 105
Fennel, Tomato, and Chicory, 106
Mixed, 107
Orange and Lemon, 104
Potato and Egg, 107-108
Romaine, 107
Squid, 105
String Bean, 106
Tomato with Orégano, 108
Salami, 29, 30, 156
Salmon, Boiled, 62
Salmone Lesso, 62
Salsa
con Acciughe, 53
con Carne, 54
con Carne e Funghi, 54
di Capperi, 53
di Funghi e Pomodoro, 55
di Piselli, 55-56
di Vongoli, 50, 57
Piccante, 55
Semplice di Pomodoro, 56
Tartufata, 57
Salsiccia
alla Griglia, 90
con Vino Rosso, 91
Sarde Beccafico, 62

SARDINES
Stuffed, 62
with Spaghetti, 47

SAUCES, 53-57
Anchovy, 53
Caper, 53
Clam, 57
Mariner, 49
Meat, 54
Meat and Mushroom, 54
Mushroom and Tomato, 55
Pea, 55
Piquant, 55
Tomato, 56
Truffle, 57
with Wine, 55, 57

SAUSAGE
Broiled, 90
Dry, 30
Pie, 149

SAUTERNE WINE, 13, 25
in Eggs *Cacciatora,* 140
with Lamb, 78

with Piquant Sauce, 55
with Rabbit, 113
with Veal, 85
Savoiardi, 132
Scaloppine alla Marsala, 84, 157
Sea Foods. *See* Fish; Shellfish
Sea Shells with Potatoes, 41
Sfinge di San Giuseppe, 17, 24, 131-32
Sgombro Ripieno, 63

SHELLFISH, 68-73. *See also* Fish; names of shellfish
Clams, 72-73
Lobster, 68-70
Oysters Mario, 72
Shrimp, 70-71
Snails, 71-72

SHERRY WINE, 13, 20, 24, 26
with Chicken, 118
with Italian Cheese Pie, 135
with Lobster, 70
with *Ossi Buchi,* 83
with Peaches, 130
with Pheasant, 114
with Pistachio Pie, 134
with Rabbit, 112, 114
with Shrimp, 70
with Squids, 59
with *Torta di Ricotta,* 135
with Trout, 68
with Truffle Sauce, 57
with Venison, 110

SHRIMP
Mario, 70-71
with Rice, 71
Sicilian Cream Tartlets, 126

SICILIAN-STYLE
Clams, 73
Cream Tart, 125
Cream Tartlets, 126
Filet Mignon, 75
Pizza, 148
Spaghetti with Fennel, 47
Snails Sicilian, 71-72
Soufflé, Tomato-*Vermicelli,* 150

SOUPS, 33-39. *See also* Broth, Fish, Meat, Vegetables
Meat, 34-36
Minestra, 38-39
Minestrone, 34, 37, 38
Nonni's, 35
Spinach with Rice, 36
Vegetable, 35, 36-39
Spada alla Griglia, 64

SPAGHETTI, 46-51. *See also Pasta*
al Burro, 47
con Acciughe, 46-47
con Melenzani, 49
con Salsa di Carne, 48
con Salsa di Vongoli, 50
con Salsa Semplice di Pomodoro, 50
e Finocchio Siciliana, 47
Marinara, 49
with Anchovy, 46-47
with Butter, 47
with Clam Sauce, 50
with Eggplant, 49
with Fennel, 47
with Mariner Sauce, 49
with Meat Sauce, 48
with Plain Sauce, 50
with Sardines, 47
Spaghettini Bagaria, 51
Sparagi Parmigiana, 103
Spiedini
alla Griglia, 84
alla Romana, 76
Veal, 84

SPINACH
Croquettes with Rice, 143
Eggs Florentine, 141
Soup with Rice, 36
Steamed, 103
Spinaci Affogati, 103
Spinola Ripiena, 65
Sponge Cake, 136, 137
Spring Menu, 25. *See also* Menus
Spumoni, 21, 22, 26, 157
Italian Ice Cream, 133

SQUASH
Fried, 104
Sweet and Sour, 103
with Lamb, 79

SQUIDS
Salad, 105
with Tomato Sauce, 59
St. Joseph's Cream Puffs, 17, 24, 131-32
St. Joseph's Day Menu, 24. *See also* Menus
St. Joseph's *Sfinge,* 17, 24, 131-32

STANDARD MEASUREMENTS, 158

STEWS
Chicken, 120
Lamb with Squash, 79
Meat, 92
Rabbit, 113
Stocco
Palermitana, 66
Sciacca, 65

STOCKFISH
Palermo, 66
Sciacca, 65

STRING BEANS
Salad, 106
Sautéed, 98
Striped Bass, 65
Suckling Pig, 81
Summer Menu, 26. *See also* Menus
Swordfish, 64

TAGLIARINI, 11, 157
con Fegatini, 51
con Sparagi, 52
with Asparagus, 52
with Chicken Livers, 51
with Fish Broth, 33

TARTS
Cassatelle, 126
Cream Puffs, 131
St. Joseph's *Sfinge,* 131

TOMATO
Salad, 106, 108
Soufflé with *Vermicelli,* 150

TOMATO SAUCE, 56
with *Ditali* Pie, 52
with *Lasagne,* 42-43
with Macaroni Muffs, 44
with *Pizza,* 149
with *Polpette,* 75
with *Ravioli,* 45-46
with Spaghetti, 50
with Stuffed Sardines, 63
with Whiting, 61
Tonno
Agro e Dolce, 66-67
alla Griglia, 67
con Salsa di Pomodoro, 67
Torta
di Ditali, 52
di Pistacchio, 21
di Ricotta, 15, 135-36
Tripe *Milanese,* 91

Trippa Milanese, 91
Trota con Acciughe, 68
Trout with Anchovy, 68
Truffle Sauce, 57
Tubettini, 11, 157
in Kidney Bean Soup, 38

TUNA FISH
Broiled, 67
Sour and Sweet, 66-67
with Tomato Sauce, 67

Uccelli Scappati, 86
Umido
di Carne, 92
di Coniglio, 113
Uova
alla Cacciatora, 140
con Olive e Provolone, 141
con Peperoni, 142
con Salsa di Pomodoro, 142
Fiorentina, 141

VEAL, 81-86
Birds, 86
Broiled Rolls, 83-84
Cacciatora, 81
Chops, Hunter's Style, 81
Costatelle Cacciatora, 81
Cotolette, 82, 153
Cutlets, 82
Ossi Buchi, 83, 155
Rollettes, 83-84
Rollini, 83-84, 156
Scaloppine, 84, 157
Shanks, 83
Spiedini, 84, 157
Uccelli Scappati, 86, 158
Vitella con Peperoni, 85-86
Vitella con Riso, 85
with Marsala, 84
with Peppers, 85-86
with Rice, 85
Vegetable-Meat Omelet, 139

VEGETABLES, 122-35. *See also* Luncheon Delicacies, Meats, names of vegetables, Salads, Soups, Spaghetti
Artichokes, 94-96
Asparagus Parmesan, 103
Broccoli, 93, 139-40
Cabbage, 80, 96-97
Cauliflower, 41
Dandelion Sautéed, 97
Eggplant, 49, 94, 100-101
Escarole, 97, 98, 105, 107
Fennel, 29, 47, 106
Mushrooms, 30, 54, 55, 87, 99
Peas with Eggs, 149-50
Peppers, 101-102
Potatoes, 37, 38, 41, 42, 88, 92, 113, 146, 147
Soufflé, 150
Spinach, 103
Squash, 79, 103-104
String Beans, 98, 106
Tomatoes, 54-57, 106, 108
Zucchini, 103-104, 158
Vegetable Soups, 36-39. *See also* Soups
Venison Mario, 110

VERMICELLI, 10, 158
Minestrone, 37
Soufflé, 150

VERMOUTH, 13, 22, 23, 25, 26
in *Zuppa Inglese,* 136
Vitella
con Peperoni, 85-86
con Riso, 85
Vongoli
Siciliana, 73
su Pane Abbrustolito, 72-73

Wedding Menu, 27. *See also* Menus

WHITING
Boiled, 60
Broth, 33
with Tomato Sauce, 61

WINES, 12-14. *See also* names of wines
correct serving of, 12-14
with Beef, 76
with Chicken, 117, 118
with Custard, 135
with Duck, 114
with Filet Mignon, 75
with Kidneys, 90
with Lamb, 78
with Liver, 87
with Lobster, 69, 70
with Peaches, 129
with Pears, 129
with Pheasant, 114
with Pork, 80
with Rabbit, 112, 113
with Sauces, 55-57
with Sausage, 91
with Shrimp, 70
with Squid, 59
with Stew, 92
with Trout, 68
with Veal, 81, 83, 84, 85
with Venison, 110
with Wild Rabbit, 113
Winter Holiday Menus, 27. *See also* Menus
Winter Menu, 26. *See also* Menus

Zabaglione, 23, 26, 135
ZUCCHINI, 103-104, 158
Dolce e Agro, 103
Fried, 104
Fritti, 104
Sweet and Sour, 103
Zuppa
di Lenticchi, 37
di Pollo, 35
di Spinaci e Riso, 36
Inglese, 27, 136-37
Vegetale con Polpettini, 35

SOUP'S ON!

☐ THE TUESDAY SOUL FOOD COOKBOOK. 200 easy-to-use recipes from *Tuesday Magazine*—with everything from black-eyed peas to pig's knuckles—in the first soul food cookbook in paperback. (PE4708—$1.00)

☐ AMERICA'S FAVORITE RECIPES FROM BETTER HOMES & GARDENS. From appetizers to luscious desserts—over 500 prize-tested recipes—275 photographs! (NE4578—95¢)

☐ HAWAII COOKBOOK & BACKYARD LUAU by Elizabeth Ahn Toupin. 175 succulent recipes plus tempting menu suggestions to turn your kitchen into an exotic tropical paradise! (SE13—75¢)

☐ James Beard's HORS D'OEUVRES & CANAPES. Great for party-giving success—sizzling taste treats and cool bite-size delights. (SE4384—75¢)

☐ THE ART OF BARBECUE COOKING. What to cook on—what to cook with—full-color photographs of many appetizing dishes—plus a special chapter on sauces. (NE4782—95¢)

☐ THE FANNIE FARMER JUNIOR COOKBOOK by Wilma Lord Perkins. The famous, illustrated guide that's been the favorite of young cooks for over two decades. (SE4677—75¢)

☐ THE COMPLETE BOOK OF MEXICAN COOKING by Elisabeth Ortiz. 340 delicious recipes in the most complete and colorful guide to Mexican cooking ever written. (NE4107—95¢)

☐ THE SPANISH COOKBOOK by Barbara Norman. Precise and simple directions for over 200 of the best recipes from the kitchens of Spain. (SE4389—75¢)

☐ AN HERB AND SPICE COOKBOOK by Craig Clairborne. The food editor of *The New York Times* presents over 400 original and tempting recipes, prepared with dozens of different herbs and spices—a subtle choice of the finest cuisines throughout the world. (SE4077—75¢)

Ask for them at your local bookseller or use this handy coupon:

BANTAM BOOKS, INC., Dept. CB, Room 300,
271 Madison Ave., N. Y., N. Y. 10016

Please mail me the Bantam Bestsellers checked above. I am enclosing $_____. (Check or money order—no currency, no C.O.D.'s please. If less than 5 books, add 10¢ per book for postage and handling.) Please allow up to four weeks for delivery.

Name_____

Address_____

City_____ State_____ Zip_____

CB—6/69

Exciting! Brand New!

Handy guides to personal success & happiness

Bantam Minibooks/50¢ each

Original books in a handy compact format— written by renowned authorities for almost every member of the family.

- ☐ TEEN HAIR AND BEAUTY CARE (FX4347)
- ☐ 101 GIFTS YOU CAN MAKE AT HOME (FX4349)
- ☐ NAME YOUR BABY (FX4345)
- ☐ YOUR FUTURE IN THE CARDS (FX4350)
- ☐ HOW TO MEET MEN (FX4346)
- ☐ KNITTING FOR BABIES (FX4356)
- ☐ HOW TO INVEST WISELY IN THE STOCK MARKET (FX4299)
- ☐ INSTANT MEMORY (FX4300)
- ☐ DAILY MEDITATIONS: YOUR GUIDE TO INNER HAPPINESS (FX4301)
- ☐ 999 DAILY NUMBERS: NUMEROLOGY (FX4302)
- ☐ THE NATURAL WAY TO BEAUTY AND HEALTH (FX4303)
- ☐ THE SIMPLE ART OF MARRIED LOVE (FX4304)
- ☐ HAIRPIECES AND WIGS (FX4205)
- ☐ DIET HATER'S DIET BOOK & GRAM COUNTER (FX4210)
- ☐ FORETELL THE FUTURE (FX4207)
- ☐ MINIBOOK OF CROSSWORD PUZZLES (FX4209)
- ☐ TEEN MODEL CALORIE COUNTER (FX4122)
- ☐ HANDBOOK & DICTIONARY OF DREAMS (FX4124)
- ☐ HANDWRITING (FX4125)
- ☐ YOGA, U.S.A. (FX4121)
- ☐ HAIRDOS AND DON'TS (FX4123)
- ☐ LEGAL RIGHTS FOR WOMEN (FX4208)
- ☐ THE MODERN WOMAN'S CONCISE MEDICAL DICTIONARY (FX4206)
- ☐ WHY DO MARRIAGES FAIL? (FX4126)

Buy them at your local bookstore or use this handy coupon:

Bantam Books, Inc., Dept. MB, Rm. 300, 271 Madison Ave., N.Y., N.Y. 10016

Please send me the merchandise I have indicated.

Name_____

Address_____

City_____ State_____ Zip_____

(Please send check or money order. No currency or C.O.D.'s. Add 10¢ per book on orders of less than 5 books to cover the cost of postage and handling.) Please allow about four weeks for delivery. MB—6/69

If you think this book was good, wait 'til you see what *else* we've got in store for you!

Send for your FREE catalog of Bantam Bestsellers today!

This money-saving catalog lists hundreds of best-sellers originally priced from $3.75 to $15.00—yours now in Bantam paperback editions for just 50¢ to $1.95! Here is a great opportunity to read the good books you've missed and add to your private library at huge savings! The catalog is FREE! So don't delay—send for yours today!

Just send us a post card with the information below or use this handy coupon:

BANTAM BOOKS, INC.
Dept. GA3, 414 East Golf Road, Des Plaines, Ill. 60016

I'm tired of paying high prices for good books. Please send me your latest free catalog of Bantam Books.

Name_____

Address_____

City_____ State_____ Zip Code_____

Please allow up to four weeks for delivery.

GA3—6/69